A RECORD OF EXCELLENCE

The Remarkable Success of
Maharishi School of the
Age of Enlightenment

Ashley Deans, Ph.D.

Maharishi University of Management Press
Fairfield, Iowa

®Maharishi School of the Age of Enlightenment, Consciousness-Based, Transcendental Meditation, Science of Creative Intelligence, TM-Sidhi, Maharishi Sthapatya Veda, Maharishi Jyotish, Maharishi Ayur-Veda, Maharishi Vedic, Maharishi Yagya, Maharishi Vedic City, Maharishi University of Management, and Transcendental Meditation-Sidhi are registered or common law trademarks licensed to Maharishi Vedic Education Development Corporation and used under sublicense or with permission.

Illustrations by Catherine Aalto
Cover design by George Foster

We gratefully acknowledge permission to use material from the following published source: Figure 3 on page 92 is adapted from Barnes V.A., Treiber F.A., and Johnson M.H. Impact of Transcendental Meditation on ambulatory blood pressure in African-American adolescents. *American Journal of Hypertension*, 17: 366-369, ©2004 American Journal of Hypertension, Ltd.

Library of Congress Cataloging-in-Publication Data

Deans, Ashley.
   A record of excellence : the remarkable success of Maharishi School of the Age of Enlightenment / Ashley Deans.
      p. cm.
   Includes bibliographical references.
   ISBN 0-923569-37-5
   1. Maharishi School of the Age of Enlightenment. 2. Education--Philosophy. 3. Transcendental meditation. I. Title.
   LD7501.F1476D43 2005
   371.04--dc22
                                        2005006815

ISBN-13: 978-0-923569-37-2
ISBN-10: 0-923569-37-5

Printed by Maharishi University of Management Press
Fairfield, Iowa 52557
www.mumpress.com
Printed in U.S.A.

Acknowledgments

I would like to thank Dr. Bevan Morris, president of Maharishi University of Management, for his inspiring leadership and for encouraging me to write this book. I am grateful to Dr. Susie Dillbeck for her helpful suggestions and to Robert Roth for his editorial assistance. Thanks also to Mario Orsatti and William Tishman for their feedback, and to Professor Fred Travis for allowing the data from his research to be adapted into the charts on pages 37 and 40. Illustrations and graphic design were provided by Catherine Aalto. Photographs were contributed by Rick Donhauser, Lin Mullenneaux, and June Oliver.

Other invaluable assistance has come from Martha Bright, Gerry Geer, and Cindy Buck, who copyedited the manuscript, and from the faculty, staff, and students of Maharishi School of the Age of Enlightenment, who contributed many comments and suggestions. Finally, I am grateful to Maharishi, the founder of Maharishi School, without whom this record of educational excellence would never have been possible.

MAHARISHI MAHESH YOGI

Founder of Maharishi School of the Age of Enlightenment, who introduced the Transcendental Meditation program to the world 50 years ago for systematically developing higher states of consciousness. Maharishi is now offering every school Consciousness-Based education so that all students everywhere can enliven total brain functioning, unfold their full creative potential, and enjoy healthy, happy, successful lives.

"The potential

of every student

is infinite.

The time of student life

should serve to unfold

that infinite potential

so that every individual

becomes a vibrant center

of Total Knowledge."

—Maharishi

Table of Contents

Introduction

Imagine you are visiting a school where there are no locks on the lockers, and pinned to a bulletin board is a five-dollar bill with a note requesting that the owner claim it.

You step into a ninth-grade classroom to be greeted by a sea of shining faces. The students are wide awake—eager to learn. You ask a question and every hand shoots up. The students giggle with anticipation.

A teacher tells you she has more energy after a day's teaching than before. A parent confides that her children complain on Fridays that there is no school on the weekend.

In the past few years the school has graduated ten times the national average of National Merit Scholar Finalists, seen 95% of graduates accepted at four-year colleges, and had grades 10–12 consistently score in the top 1% of the nation on standardized tests of educational development.

You are amazed to learn that the school has no entrance exams, with open enrollment from a diversity of backgrounds. Yet the student body is brimming with creative intelligence. Published research reports that each year students grow in intelligence, creativity, and academic performance, as well as in qualities of leadership and citizenship.

Trophy cases are overflowing with state, national, and international prizes for academics, speech, fine arts, creative problem solving, and sports. For example, in the creative problem-solving competitions Odyssey of the Mind and Destination ImagiNation, which most schools reserve for their talented and gifted program, students have won more state championships than any other school in state history. They have also won the international Global Finals three times, and garnered more top-ten finishes than any other school in the world.

And that is just the beginning. Students have won more of the top awards in group speech competitions than any other school in state history, and since they started competing in 1988, they have won 16 boys' state tennis championships—far more than any other school in that time period. Indeed, since the first graduating class in 1983, more state championship ribbons have been awarded than there are school alumni.

Perhaps even more remarkable is that these accomplishments seem to flow naturally without pressure on the students. In fact, the stress level of students and faculty is extremely low—so low that faculty have less than half the health-care costs of other schools.

Racial harmony is evident, and cliques and bullying are absent. The principal confides that he's never had to break up a fight in the past decade.

The students are obviously happy and show a deep respect for their teachers. An accreditation board member remarks that during a three-day visit he did not hear one harsh word said between any students, or between any teacher and student.

You may wonder if you are in a dream. Could a school like this really exist? The answer is yes. I'm fortunate enough to be the director of such a school, and I have written this book not because I want you to admire our achievements but so you can see how simple it is to implement what we do and replicate this success at any school anywhere.

> **You may wonder if you are in a dream. Could a school like this really exist?**

So what do we do that's different? It's very simple and the students really enjoy it. For a few minutes each day they sit comfortably and practice the Maharishi Transcendental Meditation℠ technique to develop their total creative potential. This effortless mental procedure produces holistic brain functioning, resulting in increased intelligence, reduced stress, and improved social behavior.

This book describes the success of this Consciousness-Based℠ approach to education and should be a refreshing change for those who are tired of reading books that describe in painful detail the depressing failures of modern education, but then fail to provide practical solutions.

In Chapter 1, I analyze from a new perspective the problems plaguing education, and then, in Chapter 2, I discuss a simple solution that has been scientifically verified, and field tested, in hundreds of schools around the world. In Chapters 3, 4, and 5, I describe the unique qualities of Maharishi School and the extraordinary achievements of our students. Chapter 6 reviews the unique benefits of Consciousness-Based education for the health and well-being of students and teachers, and Chapter 7 reports on the benefits seen in other schools where the program has been implemented. In Chapter 8, I present how Consciousness-Based education is being applied to prevent school violence and create a peaceful world family. Chapter 9 explains how to implement the program in any school. Chapter 10 provides new principles of education that are emerging to replace the failed old principles that have prevailed for centuries, and in conclusion, Chapter 11 gives a vision of the bright future in store for humanity as more and more schools adopt Consciousness-Based education.

The good news is that today any school can offer a practical, proven program that fulfills the highest aspirations of educators, parents, and students, simply by adding one period a day to the existing curriculum. This one addition will provide what has been lacking in education—new knowledge that is effective in solving the problems that plague our schools and society.

1

The Hazards
of Modern Education

In a first-grade class, be it inner city or private prep school, I find the students fresh and enthusiastic, literally pulling knowledge out of their teacher. They ask questions like "Why is the sky blue?" "Why do birds fly south?" or "Where do the stars go in the daytime?" But in a typical high school class, students are often sullen, frustrated, and bored. Their most likely response to a teacher who begins to expound on some point of interest will be, "Is this going to be on the test?" What is it that destroys a student's desire to know everything?

On my travels throughout North America and overseas, I often hear complaints about the failings of education. Indeed, it sometimes seems as if the only thing education doesn't lack is critics. The schools are either too rigorous or not rigorous enough. The curriculum is either too broad, failing to train students for specific jobs in the workplace, or too specialized, failing to educate students to succeed in a complex society. But the consensus is that lack of proper education is the most important factor contributing to problems in society today.

So why does education seem to be failing our children? To understand this, we should first ask what we want from education. Should it merely provide information? Or should it develop students fully and completely?

Information overload

One reason why children lose interest in school is because "information-based" education is fundamentally flawed. A child can absorb only a minute fraction of the information available in the world today, and information is more than doubling every four years. This supernova explosion of knowledge makes information-based education stressful even for the brightest students.

As Dr. John T. Wynne, vice-president emeritus of Massachusetts Institute of Technology, once told me, "Being a student at MIT is like trying to take a drink from a fire hose." This information overload swamps the student and dampens the natural desire to know more. Not surprisingly then, only about half of high school graduates manage to complete a bachelor's degree within six years,[1] and fewer than one in ten Americans over the age of 25 hold a higher degree.[2]

This low retention rate results from a system that treats the student like a container into which an ever-increasing number of facts must be crammed. But it does nothing to increase the inner capacity of the student to learn. Nothing is offered to develop such

> **As education increases its ability to deliver more information, it fails to increase the ability of the student to absorb it.**

vital qualities as clarity of mind, intelligence, creativity, memory, or inner well-being—the very qualities that make a good student!

Here lies a great weakness of information-based education. As it increases its ability to deliver more information, it fails to increase the ability of the student to absorb it. The student is left feeling overwhelmed and inadequate, and the cycle of frustration and dissatisfaction is thereby perpetuated.

The dangers of stress overload

In addition to information overload, students are bombarded with stress from excessive homework, pressure-packed examinations, lack of exercise, poor diet, and unhealthy environments. No student is immune to the epidemic of chronic stress—either in or out of school.

Stress affects both the private-school student studying for advanced placement exams and the inner-city student struggling to succeed in a hostile environment. Early morning classes are often preceded by late nights at home. Add to this such factors as family problems, social pressure, substance abuse, and stressed and burned-out teachers, and we begin to understand why education today can harm a young life.

Stress overload can lead to severe brain dysfunction and is a precursor to many diseases of mind and body, including anxiety disorders, depression, and suicide, as well as hyper-

tension and obesity in teens. Stress can even lead to "functional holes" in the brain—areas of decreased brain activity characterized by decreased cerebral blood flow and lower metabolic activity patterns. Functional holes in the brain have been associated with a wide range of behavioral problems, including attention deficit–hyperactivity disorder, substance abuse, and violence.[3]

However, education today offers little to combat the deleterious effects of stress—rather, it often promotes and perpetuates these effects. Such a system of education does not educate—it debilitates.

Stifling the desire to know

Even though the vast majority of teachers make a dedicated effort, researchers report that the classroom atmosphere is, in general, a mixture of boredom, anxiety, and cynicism.[4,5] In one study, students chose among 12 possibilities in answering the question, "What is the best thing about this school?" The top choice was "my friends;" the second was "sports activities." Among juniors and seniors, 8% chose "nothing"—an answer that turned out to be more popular than "classes I'm taking," which achieved the dismal total of 7%.[6]

Of those students who stay in school, about 40% are "just going through the motions" necessary to receive a diploma.[7] These findings confirm that, for many students, modern education is a process to be endured, rather than a joyful exploration of knowledge on the path to wisdom.

Even Einstein reported that his education dampened his enthusiasm for gaining knowledge: "One had to cram all this stuff into one's mind for the examinations, whether one liked it or not. This coercion had such a deterring effect [upon me] that, after I had passed the final examination, I found the consideration of any scientific problems distasteful to me for an entire year."[8] Clearly, fact-based education does not satisfy the desire for knowledge—it stifles it.

Even Einstein reported that his education dampened his enthusiasm for gaining knowledge.

Overspecialization

Students who continue with their education find that information overload forces them into fragmented channels of specialization. This leaves even the most brilliant minds of our scientific age working within such narrow boundaries that they may spend their entire lives exploring the neuronal structure of a snail. The result is that even Nobel Prize winners are lost outside of their own fields.

This overspecialization has led cynics to joke that gaining a Ph.D. involves learning more and more about less and less, until one ends up knowing everything about virtually nothing (as compared with many interdisciplinary

programs, where the student ends up knowing virtually nothing about everything). But joking aside, this fragmented approach has serious consequences for all of us.

A little knowledge is dangerous

If a student pilot is given partial knowledge—such as how to take off, but not how to land—the result will probably be disastrous. Similarly, the specialization of modern education guarantees that graduates will have only a partial understanding of the world around them, leading to inevitable problems.

Take scientists, for example, who have made great discoveries for the benefit of us all. However, lacking the integrated awareness necessary to comprehend the relationship between isolated laws of nature and the whole environment, they are often surprised when their new discoveries lead to unforeseen consequences. It seems that for every advance in modern science, a harmful side effect emerges, reminding us that "a little knowledge is a dangerous thing."

For instance, consider the field of agriculture. Effective pest controls such as DDT were later found to have an adverse impact on wildlife and serious implications for the health of farmers and consumers. A result of fragmented knowledge is that one man's pest control is another man's poison.

Fragmented knowledge leads to fragmented brain development

William James, the father of modern psychology, speculated that the average person uses only a small fraction of his or her full mental potential. If so, this outcome is not a glowing endorsement of conventional systems of education that only provide fragmented bits of information.

Modern neuroscience confirms that when the brain processes information, specific neuronal pathways get enlivened, but much of the brain remains uninvolved. According to neuroscientist Dr. Alarik Arenander, director of the Brain Research Institute in Iowa, "Education that provides only information about specific, fragmented, or isolated values limits the development of the student's brain, because such information processing only enlivens specific areas of the brain; it does not develop the brain physiology holistically." The result is that vast areas of brain cell networks fail to develop, and most of the brain falls victim to habitual neglect, becoming as if "junked."

> **Education that provides only information about specific, fragmented, or isolated values limits the development of the student's brain.**

Add to this the damage from stress overload and we find that, rather than providing a means to develop the total brain physiology, the teaching of fragmented knowledge leads to fragmented brain development. Of course, damaging a child's brain is certainly not the intention of any educational institution, but this is the sad reality.

Educators try to help children to develop as best they can, but even well-meaning initiatives, such as "No Child Left Behind," are still fragmented approaches. Requiring that every child read and write by grade four misses the point. After all, even a tyrant can read and write. Something new must be added to the curriculum to develop the brain holistically—otherwise, schools will continue to leave *every* child behind.

Is partial brain development normal?

Obviously, development of our total brain potential is essential if we want to enjoy success in all areas of life. Otherwise, it's like trying to run a race with our shoelaces tied together. Yet we seem to have become so accustomed to using only a small fraction of our potential that we consider it normal.

Imagine visiting an island where cars run on only one cylinder and clank along at ten miles an hour billowing black smoke. If the inhabitants know nothing else, they might think this situation is normal. However, after you produce the owner's manual and perform a tune-up, miraculously the cars run on eight cylinders, cruising at 60 mph with no visible exhaust. But this high level of performance isn't a miracle; it's simply that the cars are now using the full potential with which they were originally designed.

The problem in education today is that the owner's manual for the human brain has not been available. As a result, despite their best efforts, educators have not had the knowledge of how to "tune up" their students to achieve the higher levels of functioning of which they are capable.

In his book *The Closing of the American Mind*,[9] Allan Bloom points out that the student who approaches a university with the attitude "I am a whole human being. Help me to form myself in my wholeness and let me develop my real potential" is an embarrassment because he or she is the one to whom universities have nothing to say. If unfolding the full potential of a student has become an embarrassment, then surely the urgent need of the time is to remedy this unfortunate situation.

Holistic knowledge for holistic brain development

Indeed, fragmented knowledge restricts the development of the brain and denies students their birthright of realizing their total creative potential. Education today feeds the student with fragmented bits of information from the outside but fails to integrate these isolated facts with the personal experience of the student. Consequently, students become lost in the parts of knowledge and do not experience the unified basis of all knowledge. This leaves them unable to fathom the relationship between what they are learning and themselves. The result is widespread dissatisfaction with education and inevitable problems for the individual and society.

So what is the solution? How can we provide holistic knowledge that satisfies the student and develops the holistic functioning of the brain? The answer is that in addition to providing knowledge from the outside, education should unfold knowledge from the inside. This new approach turns the current understanding of what education should be inside-out, so to speak.

Leading out total creative potential from within

Looking within for the source of holistic knowledge is not a new idea. An inscription on the Delphic Oracle in ancient Greece exhorted seekers of truth to "know thyself," but in this modern age, students wanting to "find themselves" can expect to be greeted with bewilderment and to receive no clear direction as to how to proceed.

Some insight into the ideal of education may be gained by considering the origin of the word *education*, which derives from the Latin *educere*— to lead out. This principle is opposite to modern education, which doesn't lead out—it crams in.

Education in its deepest sense should involve more than merely an attempt to supply ever-increasing volumes

> *Education* derives from the Latin *educere*—to lead out. This principle is opposite to modern education, which doesn't lead out— it crams in.

of information, which we could call *the known*. To be successful, education must provide a means to develop the student's innate creative intelligence—*the knower*. Without a means to develop the knower, education can never provide complete knowledge of the known. After all, if a student doesn't know himself, then what else can he reliably know?

For education to be complete, it must provide the three elements necessary for complete knowledge:

1. Develop the total creative potential of the knower

2. Fully enliven all aspects of the process of knowing

3. Provide complete knowledge of the known

It is time for a return to the original purpose of education—*educere*—to lead out the infinite creative potential inherent within everyone. Fortunately today, a simple technique to accomplish this is available.

In the following chapter, I will present the key to unfolding the total creative potential of the student—the Maharishi Transcendental Meditation technique, which offers a practical, proven means to develop the holistic functioning of the total brain physiology. By providing students with the experience of Transcendental Consciousness, education can rise from offering only partial knowledge of the known to offering complete knowledge of the knower, process of knowing, and the known. In this way, education can rise from offering "all knowledge in every campus" to culturing "all knowledge in every brain."

2

Developing the Total Creative Potential of the Student

In January 1973, I was in Alaska studying the aurora borealis for my doctorate in physics at York University, Toronto. The research involved long nights observing the upper atmosphere with sophisticated ground-based instruments, and months preparing rocket payloads to be launched high into space. It was on a chilly sub-zero day, with the sun struggling to rise above the horizon, that I received a letter from an old school friend, telling me he had learned the Transcendental Meditation technique and that I would really enjoy it. Little did I know that my interests were about to turn from outer space to inner space.

In April 1973, I returned to Toronto from Alaska and attended two lectures on the Transcendental Meditation (TM®) program of Maharishi Mahesh Yogi. I didn't know quite what to expect. A pleasant, well-dressed young man welcomed the audience and gave a short talk on what would be involved in learning the technique.

He told us that the practice is effortless, does not

involve contemplation or concentration, and requires no change in lifestyle, philosophy, or religious belief. He explained that the technique comes from the ancient Vedic* science of consciousness.

The course of instruction would be held over four consecutive days, for about an hour and a half each day. Then, he said, we would be accomplished meditators and could meditate at home for 15 to 20 minutes in the morning and evening.

The lectures stirred my interest, so the following Saturday morning I turned up at the Transcendental Meditation center for instruction. I was taught the technique, and after a few minutes I was deeply relaxed, and my mind was peaceful, yet alert. I was astonished how easy it was to experience this silent, pleasant state of inner awareness.

Within a few days, I noticed that I had more energy, that I was better able to focus on my studies, and that I was more cheerful in general. I wished that I had learned this technique in grade school.

The Transcendental Meditation technique— simple, natural, effortless

Now, over 30 years later, I find myself running a school where all the students practice the Transcendental Meditation program. When visitors to the school see a class meditating, they often ask, "What are they doing?"

---

* *Vedic*, derived from the Sanskrit word *Veda*, means *pertaining to Total Knowledge*.

I explain that the Transcendental Meditation technique is so simple that it can be learned by anyone—even children. It is easier than learning ABC's in kindergarten. It utilizes the natural tendency of the mind to seek something more charming—a familiar experience to any student who has tried to study in a library, only to find that his or her attention has shifted to some beautiful music wafting up from a concert on the lawn outside.

Like a diver who takes the correct angle, lets go, and dives into the water, the mind naturally dives

The Transcendental Meditation technique is an effortless means to experience the reservoir of total creative potential deep within everyone.

within to the field of greatest charm, the ocean of inner happiness that is *Transcendental Consciousness* at the source of thought.

The Transcendental Meditation technique is an effortless means to experience the reservoir of total creative potential deep within everyone. And just as a diver comes out of the water saturated and refreshed after a dive, the mind of the meditator becomes saturated with creative intelligence, alert and refreshed, ready to support dynamic, successful activity.

Are our students fully awake?

Have you ever had the experience of walking into a classroom on a Monday morning? If so, you will have no problem recognizing that students display different states of consciousness. The back row may be sleeping—a state where no amount of creative lesson planning on your part can motivate them to learn. The students in the middle rows may be dreaming. Hopefully, in the front row, the students are awake, showing a keen interest in what the teacher is teaching. Doesn't every teacher wish that students could all be "front-rowers"—fully awake and eager for knowledge?

This increased receptivity is what the Transcendental Meditation technique develops. It provides a natural means to "wake up" the students to states of heightened alertness—higher states of consciousness.

The missing element in education

Today thousands of students around the world are developing higher states of consciousness because they are attending schools where the Transcendental Meditation technique is offered as part of the curriculum. Jennie Rothenberg, a National Merit Scholar, attributes her success to her ability to "dive within to the source of thought." Jennie explains, "For me the most practical benefit of Transcendental Meditation is physiological—it keeps me rested. I have less stress, and I'm more coherent. I will go to school, sit down, and meditate for 15 minutes, and it is so refreshing. I feel afterwards that I've rested for about eight hours. I am so alert I can function much better in my school-work and extracurricular activities."

How does Jennie get these benefits? Not by reading a book, or by memorizing the periodic table of chemical elements, or by knowing how to solve a quadratic equation, but simply by diving within and *experiencing* the source of thought. It is this experience of the source of thought—the source of the ABC's—the source from where all knowledge sprouts—that develops the total creative potential of the knower, engaging and enlivening the whole brain and refreshing the physiology.

Imagine if every student were like Jennie: fresh and rested, with less stress, and enjoying a greater sense of self. The classrooms of the world would be culturing students to develop higher states of consciousness and to express their boundless creative intelligence, rather than acting as a breeding ground for stress and dissatisfaction.

Higher states of consciousness

Let's consider for a moment the idea of higher states of consciousness. All of us are familiar with three states of consciousness: waking, dreaming, and sleeping. A physiologist can determine which state of consciousness you are in because each state has unique physical and mental correlates. For example, deep sleep produces very slow brain wave patterns (as measured by an electroencephalogram or EEG), slow breathing, and no awareness. Dreaming is associated with high-frequency brain waves (beta waves) and rapid eye movements (REM); if you were to be awakened from this state, you would probably report some illusory awareness—maybe being chased by a tiger.

The waking state exhibits brain wave patterns that are similar to those during dreaming, but waking is associated with greater metabolic activity and awareness of the external surroundings. It can be said to be a "higher" state of consciousness than sleeping or dreaming because awareness in waking is more comprehensive than in the other two states.

In March 1970, Dr. Robert Keith Wallace at Harvard University published research in *Science*[10] reporting that the Transcendental Meditation program naturally and effortlessly provides the experience of a fourth major state of consciousness—Transcendental Consciousness. Dr. Wallace described this newly discovered state as a state of "restful alertness," physiologically distinct from waking, sleeping, or dreaming. Dr. Wallace was the first to show that this fourth state of consciousness is characterized by an increase in medium-frequency alpha brain-wave activity and by a more coherent, holistic style of brain functioning. At the same time, the physiology experiences a deep state of rest.

This was the state of consciousness I experienced on the day I was instructed in Toronto. My body was deeply rested, but at the same time I was awake inside. Indeed, I was more aware than I had ever been before.

The importance of the fourth state of consciousness

The heightened alertness accompanying the experience of Transcendental Consciousness, together with its more integrated physiological characteristics, would classify it as a higher state of consciousness—higher than waking, sleeping, or dreaming. Just as it is detrimental to be deprived of sleeping or dreaming, deprivation of the fourth state of consciousness—Transcendental Consciousness—results in partial brain development and the accumulation of deeply rooted stresses and strains in the physiology.

Imagine you were marooned on a desert island where no one slept. The inhabitants would doubtless be extremely irritable. If you told them about sleep, and explained that sleep was a natural experience that would do them good, they could well be skeptical.

Some might argue, "We are so busy; how can we afford to spend a third of our lives doing nothing—just sleeping?"

> **Just as it is detrimental to be deprived of sleeping or dreaming, deprivation of Transcendental Consciousness— the fourth state of consciousness— results in partial brain development.**

But once they had experienced sleep and enjoyed the benefits, the new routine would soon be adopted by everyone. Research on the inhabitants would find distinct physiological changes during sleep, along with immediate improvements in mental and physical health, together with more harmonious social behavior.

The kind of initial response described above is not unlike the one Maharishi received when he first arrived in America in 1959. Levels of stress and anxiety in the country were high, and his teaching that great benefits

> **Only the experience of Transcendental Consciousness enlivens the total brain physiology.**

would result from the experience of a fourth major state of consciousness, effortlessly available through the Transcendental Meditation technique, was certainly a new concept.

Some argued, "We are so busy; how can we afford to spend 15 to 20 minutes twice a day meditating?" But some people tried it and immediately experienced greater well-being. The deep relaxation enjoyed during the practice of the Transcendental Meditation technique naturally dissolved the harmful effects of stress. As a result they became less anxious and more alert during daily activity.

Scientists, such as Dr. Wallace, measured distinct physiological changes and began reporting profound benefits in the areas of mental potential, health, and social behavior. Now, it is widely recognized that the Transcendental Meditation technique provides the natural experience of a fourth state of consciousness that had previously been overlooked and forgotten. And perhaps most significant for education is the finding that only the experience of Transcendental Consciousness enlivens the total brain physiology.[11,12] (See Figure 1.)

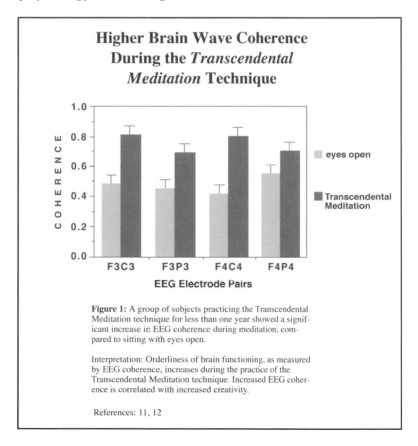

Figure 1: A group of subjects practicing the Transcendental Meditation technique for less than one year showed a significant increase in EEG coherence during meditation, compared to sitting with eyes open.

Interpretation: Orderliness of brain functioning, as measured by EEG coherence, increases during the practice of the Transcendental Meditation technique. Increased EEG coherence is correlated with increased creativity.

References: 11, 12

What science has discovered about the Transcendental Meditation program

Since 1970, over 600 scientific research studies performed at more than 200 universities and research institutes in over 30 countries have reported a wide range of benefits resulting from the practice of the Transcendental Meditation technique. (See Bibliography.) Reported benefits include the following:

Development of Full Mental Potential

- Increased creativity, intelligence, and learning ability
- Higher levels of brain functioning
- Improvements in academics and school behavior
- Benefits for special and remedial education

Improved Physical and Mental Health

- Reduced cardiovascular disease risk factors
- Decreased medical care utilization and hospitalization
- Decreased anxiety and faster recovery from stress
- Reversal of aging and increased longevity

Improved Social Behavior

- Increased efficiency
- Improved integration of personality
- Reduced substance abuse
- Effective criminal rehabilitation
- Reduced crime and conflict
- Improved economic and social trends

The benefits described in these research findings are unprecedented in their scope. Clearly, the regular experience of the fourth state of consciousness nurtures a level of mind–body integration that makes so-called "normal" human development seem severely stunted in comparison.

Research shows that benefits are immediate and cumulative. Over time, the brain physiology functions more coherently (see Figure 2) even during activity[11,12] and sleep.[13] This increasing integration and unity of brain functioning indicates the growth of higher states of consciousness culminating in *Unity Consciousness**—the state of full enlightenment, where the brain exhibits global EEG coherence and the student lives his or her total creative potential at all times.

> **Regular experience of Transcendental Consciousness nurtures a level of mind–body integration that makes so-called "normal" human development seem severely stunted in comparison.**

---

* Maharishi has brought to light that there are seven states of consciousness. These are sleeping, dreaming, waking, Transcendental Consciousness, Cosmic Consciousness, God Consciousness, and Unity Consciousness.

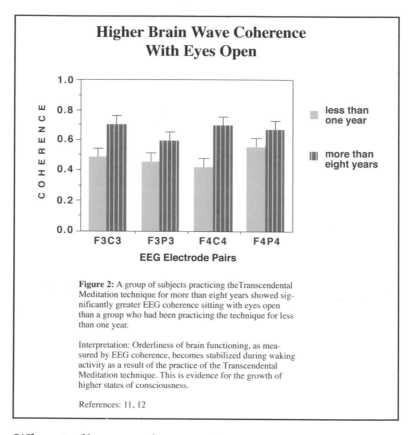

Figure 2: A group of subjects practicing theTranscendental Meditation technique for more than eight years showed significantly greater EEG coherence sitting with eyes open than a group who had been practicing the technique for less than one year.

Interpretation: Orderliness of brain functioning, as measured by EEG coherence, becomes stabilized during waking activity as a result of the practice of the Transcendental Meditation technique. This is evidence for the growth of higher states of consciousness.

References: 11, 12

Who studies consciousness?

Now you may ask, "Who studies consciousness, creativity, and intelligence?" Surely psychologists would study consciousness and intelligence as part of their effort to understand the human mind. Psychologists have certainly developed batteries of tests to determine if one person is more intelligent or creative than another; yet they don't seem to have developed any systematic means of significantly increasing creativity and intelligence over a period of time. If they had, that approach would be taught in schools—wouldn't it?

While some psychologists may be studying consciousness, this pursuit appears to be somewhat peripheral to the mainstream. A visit to the website of the American Psychological Association reveals more than 50 divisions of the Association, such as family psychology, educational psychology, and developmental psychology, but no division that studies consciousness itself. Indeed, the head of a psychology department at a university in Montreal told me in confidence that he thought psychologists didn't know any more about the fundamental nature of consciousness today than they did a hundred years ago.

Does medicine have a better handle on consciousness through its specialty of psychiatry? In reality, psychiatry is primarily concerned with the treatment of mental health disorders, using therapies such as counseling and psychotropic drugs, rather than with the development of consciousness.

At one lecture I gave on the Transcendental Meditation program to psychiatrists at a university hospital, the department head expressed an interest in learning to meditate. He confessed that he himself had been undergoing psychiatric analysis for 15 years, but he didn't think it was working very well. The knowledge that developing higher states of consciousness was easy and effortless was a breath of fresh air for him and his colleagues.

Would philosophers have a better handle on what consciousness is? Apparently not. Philosophy, it has been said, is "talk about talk."[14] But talking about consciousness occurs in the waking state (until you start to doze off). Talk does not provide the experience of Transcendental Consciousness. Without this experience, talk about consciousness is baseless.

It is hardly surprising, therefore, that universities offer courses with titles such as "The Problem of Consciousness." Such courses consider a wide range of philosophical ideas about consciousness but provide no consensus as to what consciousness actually is. Hence, consciousness has been labeled a "problem."

The Science of Creative Intelligence® (SCI)

The lack of a discipline devoted to the study of consciousness led Maharishi to found a new science—the Science of Creative Intelligence (SCI). While modern science studies laws of nature (i.e., organizing principles of intelligence) such as gravity and electromagnetism, only SCI studies consciousness, or intelligence, itself. SCI explores the intelligence of the knower, the full range of the known, and the relationship between the two.

SCI is unique in two ways. First, it provides theoretical insight into the nature of creative intelligence, as expressed in the life of the student and in the universe around us. Second, through the Transcendental Meditation program, it provides a systematic technique to allow students to experience the source of thought, the unified foundation of their own intelligence—the Self. This is experienced as the Unified Field of all the Laws of Nature—the unified basis of the intelligent principles that govern the universe as a whole. (See Appendix I.)

Unlike other sciences, which many students find diffi-cult and try to avoid, SCI is easy and enjoy-able because students directly experience their own Self. They can appreciate the con-nection between their own intelligence and the intelligence expressed throughout nature. Says high school junior Melinda Schindler, "The Science of Creative Intelligence takes basic principles of life and shows how there is a unified wholeness underlying the diversity of the world. SCI allows me to connect everything together by giving me the experience that the various academic dis-ciplines are all expressions of my own intelligence."

Melinda
Schindler

Benefits for students

SCI is enjoyable because it explores the total range of knowledge: both objective and subjective. Objectively, it studies the total range of the universe around us—from the infinite diversity expressed by billions of galaxies to the Unified Field at their basis. Subjectively, through the Transcendental Meditation technique, it researches the total range of the universe within us—from the activity of the surface level of thought to the silence of the Unified Field at the source of thought. Inner research into this total range of knowledge increases the creativity and intelli-gence of the student.

In contrast, modern scientists find that their research is often frustrating, being 1% inspiration and 99% perspiration.

Furthermore, modern science explores only partial knowledge and may actually decrease creativity and intelligence because of the stress involved.

Fortunately, if intellectual focus is alternated with the experience of the source of thought—the field of pure intelligence—the brain develops holistically, resulting in the experience of bliss rather than strain.

A study published in the journal *Intelligence*[15] found that students who had learned the Transcendental Meditation technique six months earlier had, compared with controls, increased significantly in creativity, fluid intelligence, and practical intelligence, and had decreased in levels of anxiety.

Consciousness-Based education

Growing interest in the Transcendental Meditation technique and the Science of Creative Intelligence has led to a rising demand for a system of education that develops the total creative potential of the student and prevents the harmful effects of stress. This demand has inspired Maharishi to develop a program for schools and universities—

Consciousness-Based education.

Consciousness-Based education is very easy to implement. As we will see in subsequent chapters, students simply sit in their chairs in the classroom and practice the Transcendental Meditation technique for a few

> **Consciousness-Based education is very easy to implement in schools.**

minutes twice a day. The effects are immediate.

Michael Fredrickson, a high school valedictorian, reported, "It's great to be able to practice Transcendental Meditation at the beginning of the day to get you ready for the rest of the day. When I'm more alert, and have less stress, my classes are a lot easier." This experience is typical of the hundreds of thousands of students attending schools all over the world where Consciousness-Based education is offered.

Michael
Fredrickson

In the next chapter, I will introduce you to the flagship school of Consciousness-Based education, Maharishi School of the Age of Enlightenment, where I have been the director since 1991. This chapter will give you a glimpse of what the future can be like when students have the opportunity to develop their full creative potential.

3

Maharishi School: A Model for *Consciousness-Based* Education

I feel fortunate to be the director of Maharishi School, where the benefits of Consciousness-Based education are obvious for all to see. I don't know what I expected when I first started working here. Somehow I had thought that a school with 500 children would be noisy, but I remember being surprised by the silence. Not a dull silence, but the lively, dynamic silence radiated by students who are on task, focused on gaining knowledge, happy in themselves, and enjoying extraordinary success.

Maharishi School of the Age of Enlightenment is a special place in the world. A member of the National Association of Independent Schools, it is accredited by the Independent Schools Association of the Central States, the North Central Association of Colleges and Schools, and the Iowa Department of Education (K–6).

Located on the grounds of Maharishi University of Management* in Fairfield, Iowa, the campus looks like

*See Appendix II.

a typical school, with a three-story red-brick building shaded by tall trees. But it doesn't take long to realize that this school is far from ordinary.

A day begins

It's 8:20 a.m., and children are scurrying through the school's east entrance. They make their way to the meditation halls—one for boys, one for girls—which we call the "Halls of Bliss." There they sit comfortably, ready to start meditating.

It always amazes guests to see our students chattering away with each other one minute and sinking into deep silence the next. You could hear a pin drop at this time of day. Even the eighth-grade boys sit serenely with a glow on their faces as they meditate.

"How do you get teenagers to sit quietly for 15 minutes?" is a question I am often asked. The answer is: the Transcendental Meditation technique is so enjoyable that students settle into the blissful silence at the source of thought in a very natural way.

Sheer-el Cohen

Sheer-el Cohen, whose parents emigrated from Israel just so he could attend our high school, says, "I like the fact that we have our Transcendental Meditation program in a group together. It creates a great harmony among the students."

After 15 minutes, students head off to class. The courses

they take are similar to those offered in many other schools. Students study the usual subjects—math, science, language arts, social studies, etc. The main addition to the curriculum is that the practice of the Transcendental Meditation technique is structured into the routine, together with one period a day for the Science of Creative Intelligence. Could adding something as simple as this really make that much difference?

> "The students at Maharishi School, from kindergarten to the upper grades, have the longest attention span of any I have seen in my 30 years of teaching and educational research."

After a two-day visit, Dr. Charles Mathews, formerly a professor of science education at Florida State University, told me, "The students at Maharishi School, from kindergarten to the upper grades, have the longest attention span of any I have seen in my 30 years of teaching and educational research."

This observation is even more remarkable in light of the school's open enrollment policy. There are no entrance exams, aptitude tests, or academic performance requirements. In fact, we admit virtually every student who applies.

Yet, even though children enroll with a wide range of

abilities, teachers uniformly report that the classes are unlike any they have ever experienced. "I have taught school for 22 years, including children at the laboratory school of UCLA and the Stanford University Elementary School," says Roxie Teague. "The students at Maharishi School are the most exceptional I have ever had. With their ability to focus in classroom instruction, they learn things the first time."

Academic excellence

The improved learning ability that our children exhibit is reflected by research published in the journal *Education*,[16,17] which reported that new students at Maharishi School show significant improvements in academic achievement on standardized tests within one academic year.

Devi Mays

Compared with other schools, grade-level scores on standardized tests improve significantly each year, culminating in a "topping out" at the 99th percentile by grade 10. In fact, grades 10–12 consistently score in the 99th percentile on the Iowa Tests of Educational Development (ITED), both nationally and in Iowa.

National Merit Scholar Devi Mays finds that the Transcendental Meditation program not only helps her academically but also adds to her enjoyment of life. "Maharishi School has contributed to my success in so many areas, but

Emily Marcus

Transcendental Meditation has helped especially. When I meditate I feel so much bliss. It allows me to focus so much more. That has helped me in my academics and throughout my life. I come out of meditation knowing that everything is going to be fine."

Emily Marcus, National Merit Scholar Finalist, graduated with over 25% of her senior class recognized as either National Merit Scholar Finalists or National Merit Commended Scholars. She attributes her success to her ability to focus on her studies while maintaining a settled state of mind. "It's as if the knowledge from the teacher is absorbed into the silent pool of my awareness and remains there undisturbed for me to retrieve it whenever I need to."

Maharishi School has graduated over ten times the national average of National Merit Scholar Finalists in the past five years. More than 95% of graduates are accepted at four-year colleges, and in recognition of this achievement, the school is one of only five to be granted College Preparatory status by the State of Iowa.

> **More than 95% of graduates are accepted at four-year colleges.**

Patrick Bassett, currently president of the National Association of Independent Schools in Washington, D.C., has commented, "Maharishi School is routinely recognized as outstanding in Iowa, since its students frequently take top prizes in statewide academic competitions. It is a world-renowned independent school of the highest caliber academically. "

Indeed, since the first high school graduating class of seven seniors in 1985, over 600 state championship ribbons have been won, either individually or by members of a team, for academic and extracurricular activities, not to mention numerous national and international honors. But before I describe these achievements in more detail, I would like to introduce you to another unique feature of Maharishi School—the ideal learning environment.

Peaceful and creative atmosphere

Visitors often remark on how calm, peaceful, and safe our school is. For example, a TV camera crew reported that our students had no locks on their lockers. Our students flourish in this nurturing environment. Aditya Jones, a Maharishi School alumna currently studying for a career in medicine, remembers the school as "a very friendly and peaceful place." Volleyball standout Joy Grant concurs: "The environ-

Aditya Jones

ment at the School is coherent. It's like one big happy family. I feel I know everyone and I feel comfortable with everyone."

When Iowa Teacher of the Year Jill Olsen-Virlee visited us, she clearly recognized what we have created. "Your school was truly an inspiration. The inner peace, the concern for one another, the respect and thirst for wisdom, and a holistic approach to children are awesome," she wrote after her visit.

> **"Your school was truly an inspiration. The inner peace, the concern for one another, the respect and thirst for wisdom, and a holistic approach to children are awesome."**

"I find the atmosphere at Maharishi School to be truly unique amongst schools—an ideal atmosphere for learning," said Dr. Ichak Adizes, an international management consultant who visited our school. "I was overwhelmed by the peacefulness on one hand, the level of creativity on the other hand. The peaceful creativity at Maharishi School is awesome. You never see both together."

First impressions

Students who transfer from other schools immediately notice the different atmosphere. Orion Abrams, who transferred from a public school system, recalls the contrast with his previous school. "People at Maharishi School are a lot nicer and more loving. They communicate with each other on a deeper level than a curt, judgmental, 'You do this.' At Maharishi School we really connect with each other deeply."

The parent of another transfer student, visiting for the first time, told me, "Just by the brightness of the students' faces, I can see you have created a miracle here."

Another transfer student, Jennifer

"The quality of the students, the quality of their hearts and minds, just seemed to shine in the radiant beauty of their faces."

Maidment, says, "When I attended my local public high school, I started every day with a knot of anxiety and apprehension in my stomach. When I entered Maharishi School as a sophomore, I felt as if I was in a dream—the teachers were kind and compassionate, and the students were instantly accepting and inclusive. What a difference!"

Janet Thomas, who teaches literature, recalls her first impression of Maharishi School: "I'll never forget the first day that I arrived. I had been teaching at top private schools in Australia, and the first thing that struck me when I walked into the School was that every student looked radiant. The quality of the students, the quality of their hearts and minds, just seemed to shine in the radiant beauty of their faces."

One of the many pluses of my job is that I have become accustomed to comments like these from teachers who come in contact with our students. "They are always so cooperative and conscientious about doing a good job. They are very polite, and that is unusual these days," a local high school teacher remarked when he taught classes in driver's education at Maharishi School.

Senior educators notice things that nowadays may seem out of fashion. "When I asked a question, everyone raised their hand," said a visiting principal. "Seeing children stand when called upon to speak is good for these old bones," remarked an accreditation team member. Another told me, "I haven't heard a harsh word between any students, or between any student and faculty, during the entire three days I've been here."

This is the nourishing atmosphere I work in every day. It is not a miracle. It results from the Transcendental Meditation program's ability to reduce stress and anxiety in the lives of the students and teachers and to promote more harmonious behavior.

With Consciousness-Based education, I see children spontaneously blossoming into successful, integrated individuals who feel at home with everyone and everything. Maharishi School alumnus Jivan Hall, now a successful businessman in New York City, says, "I really appreciate the strong foundation that was laid during my years at Maharishi School and the inner strength that I draw upon daily in this fast-paced, high-tech world."

These successful young men and women are shining examples of the benefits to be derived from Consciousness-Based education. Scientists have long debated whether nature (our genes) or nurture (our upbringing and environment) is more influential in making us the individuals that we are. The success of these students, taken together with the benefits reported in research findings on the Transcendental Meditation technique, brings to light the importance of the nature of the nurture our youth receive.

Jivan Hall

With their growth toward higher states of consciousness resulting in greater achievement in daily life, these students enjoy 200% value of life—100% inner fulfillment and 100% outer success—as we shall see in the following chapter.

4

Record of Excellence: Achievements of Maharishi School Students

One of the highlights of my job is watching our students perform, whether it be at a science fair, at a math bee, in the theater, or in the sports arena. When I attend these events, teachers and administrators from other schools often ask me why we are so successful. At the state drama festival, they ask me if we are a theater school. At the science fair, they ask if we are a science academy. At creativity competitions, such as Odyssey of the Mind, they ask if we spend time solving the problems in school. I reply that the students work on their projects as extracurricular activities. At the state tennis tournament, I have been asked if we run a tennis academy. An art school? A photography studio? And so it goes on. Now let me tell you some stories about our students whom I consider to be the most integrated, eloquent, and creative in the world.

Math with smiles—not anxiety

Math appears to be the only subject with its own syndrome—math anxiety. Many students struggle with math, and less than 1% of high school graduates major in math at college. In contrast, our students enjoy doing math.

I remember the time I was taking some visitors to see the sixth-grade girls' class. When we arrived, we discovered the girls were having a birthday celebration in a classroom down the hall. My guests were astonished to see how eagerly the class ended their party and hurried back to their classroom so they could explain what they had been learning that day in math. Reviewing the math lesson seemed to be more fun for them than the party.

So whatever happened to math anxiety? In contrast to what I have observed at other schools, our students always seem to look at the world from a fresh perspective that allows them to enjoy the process of finding solutions to problems, without anxiety about whether they will succeed or not. The result is that math becomes fun.

Ted Hirsch

It also becomes easier. When Ted Hirsch, who was on the school's state championship golf team, was approached by his math teacher to compete in the American High School Math Exam, he couldn't take the idea seriously at first. "I didn't really think I was anything special at math," says Ted. "I never expected to be able to do any of the problems. But I found that with a bit of thought they really weren't so hard. It amazed me when it was announced that our team had come first in the state." Ted was so inspired by the experience he decided to major in math in college.

This is the kind of example I see every day when our students put their attention on something. Their thought processes are so flexible that they quickly adapt to new challenges. Consciousness-Based education develops such clarity of mind that mathematics becomes almost effortless.

> **Consciousness-Based education develops such clarity of mind that mathematics becomes almost effortless.**

Upper School math teacher Laurie Eyre has noticed that while not every student is a mathematical genius, every student does develop a deeper appreciation for the subtler principles of mathematics. She reports, "Mathematics is the language of order and precision. Because Transcendental Meditation imbues the student's mind with the experience of pure consciousness—the silent source of order and precision in nature—students can more easily appreciate the big picture of what is going on in a math problem. They are able to perceive more of the wholeness and to cognize the underlying patterns, making it easier for them to decide which rules to apply in a given situation."

The proof of this can be seen by the fact that Maharishi

School students consistently win competitions in mathematics, such as MathCounts and Math Bee, and have represented the State of Iowa at the National MathCounts Competition. Upper School math teacher George Kelley, who coached the students for the American High School Math Exam, says, "Maharishi School students are quite extraordinary. We have been ranked first in the state in this exam for four years in a row. This is very fulfilling for me as a teacher."

Given open enrollment, and no entrance exams, Maharishi School teachers have to engage students who have a wide range of mathematical abilities. They succeed because Consciousness-Based education offers a previously missing ingredient to math education—the holistic development of the brain. This is the basis for success not only in mathematics but also in all areas of life.

Theater arts

Maharishi School students also excel in speech and drama. Each year approximately 24,000 Iowa students start out at the district level from over 300 schools, vying for a coveted invitation to the Iowa High School Speech Association Large Group Festival. Only about 100 of these schools will have groups chosen to perform at the All-State Festival.

At the festival, these lucky few will compete for the honor of "Critic's Choice," the top performance in the state of Iowa, selected by a judge who is a professional in the field. Performance areas include one-act play, choral reading, musical theater, readers' theater, group and solo mime, ensemble acting, TV newscasting, radio broadcasting, and group improvisation.

One of my favorite events is choral reading, an event involving up to 15 students. Over a period of several months, students research literature on their chosen theme, create a script, and then read it. As the name implies, choral elements are included, but these must not dominate over the spoken word. The maximum length of the piece is 15 minutes.

Because of its popularity, this event usually takes place in a large hall such as the host school's gymnasium. The acoustics are usually cavernous, putting extra pressure on the teams to enunciate with precision and project to the top of the packed bleachers.

One of Maharishi School's winning entries, which I remember well, was entitled "The Geography of Yearning." As our group prepared to begin, the gymnasium filled, the doors closed, and a hushed anticipation permeated the atmosphere. The students, dressed as nineteenth-century explorers, began to fill the air with "a cacophonous echolalia" of jungle sounds emanating from ten, then one, then all fifteen voices in perfect synchrony. A whisper filled the air: "We have reached our embarcadero."

Every scene created a unique mood, each subtly revealing the yearning of the human spirit for profound knowledge, greater understanding, and the dawn of wisdom.

The faces of the audience reflected their deep appreciation as the ensemble blended together and then separated, unified and diversified within the chosen theme. Alternating sound with silence, the students transformed the stuffy atmosphere, bathed in artificial lights, into an experience of wonder.

I remember one of the judges remarking at the end of the performance, "I wish I could just sit in silence without having to comment." Teachers and parents from different schools came up to congratulate me. A typical comment was, "Your students are so wholesome. What is it that makes them stand out?" I overheard a mother talking with her friend as they left. "Maybe it's because they have a class every day devoted to speech," she said, to which her friend replied, "Maybe it's because this meditation thing really works."

"Your students are so wholesome. What is it that makes them stand out?"

Gerald Swanson, a business executive who has sent three children to our school, remarked that this was the second year he had seen our students perform and now he realized what was special—it was the children themselves. "It's as if you can see their 'Self' when they perform," he said.

Students from other schools congratulated the performers: "We respect you guys so much; we try to imitate your stuff, but it just doesn't work." What is this intangible quality that everyone sees but no one can express? Another judge remarked, "Excellence incarnate. Every movement was polished to perfection—every song, every gesture, was just right. A magnificent performance. I didn't want to take my eyes off you to write any comments. Wonderful—very enjoyable."

Among the judges' comments, perhaps the following came closest to defining the intangible: "You all have very bright faces. You all exude so much attitude; it's a joy to watch you." This judge had noticed the radiance from within that I see every day—bright eyes, clear skin, radiant health, and pure wholesomeness. "You are all so good-looking; I suppose that's a prerequisite for admission to your school," another judge commented.

These qualities cannot be taught in speech class or in language arts or be acquired from a math or chemistry book. This brightness emanates from a healthy physiology, which expresses rising states of consciousness within. It is the liveliness of the field of creative intelligence within our students that radiates from their faces, brings sweetness to their speech, and spontaneously generates friendliness and compassion in their souls. As one judge remarked to an ensemble of Maharishi School freshmen, "I can't believe you're only in ninth grade. There are some beautiful people here."

Award-winning theater arts teacher Rodney Franz finds that Maharishi School students have a broader awareness:

"Because the students at Maharishi School have enlarged the 'container of knowledge,' their perspective is larger. They see things in terms of wholeness. It is a wonderful thing for a director to have young actors and performers who are seeing the world through a wide-angle lens."

Even though we only started competing in 1988, Maharishi School has won more "Critic's Choice" awards than any other school in the history of the state. Chuck Offenberger, longtime columnist for *The Des Moines Register*, attended the Iowa High School Speech Association event out of curiosity one year

> **Maharishi School has won more "Critic's Choice" awards than any other school in the history of the state.**

and saw Maharishi School walk off with the trophy awarded to the school judged to have the highest number of outstanding performances in the state that year. Offenberger wrote in his column, "When it comes to competition in the arts and the more genteel sports—tennis, running, golf, and the like—are the Maharishi kids taking over or what?"

Chuck Offenberger's comments reveal that these students don't just excel in one area—they can do anything they put their minds to.

The most creative students in the world

I love to go and watch our students compete in Odyssey of the Mind and Destination ImagiNation. These are creative problem-solving competitions, which have grown to include participants from all 50 states and over 20 countries.

At many schools, these activities are only offered as part of a program for talented and gifted students. However, at Maharishi School, any student may participate. Students work in teams over a period of several months to develop a creative solution to a prescribed problem.

Some problems require the use of engineering skills to construct lightweight balsa-wood structures that will support hundreds of pounds of weight. Others may require the design of remote-controlled, motorized vehicles that must negotiate an obstacle course.

Maharishi School teams have had more top-ten finishes at the international finals than any other school in the world.

Since beginning the program in 1994, Maharishi School has won 41 state championships in Odyssey of the Mind and Destination ImagiNation—more than any other school in the state. As state champions, our teams have gone on to represent Iowa at the international finals, where Maharishi School has won the Global Finals of Destination Imagination three times and had more top-ten finishes than any other school in the world.

Coach Mark Headlee is enthusiastic about "the amazing creativity and organizing power these children display." He says, "When our students go to competitions and perform, many judges have commented on the natural poise that they express. In contrast, other students need to take classes in how to be poised in front of an audience. Our students have the natural ability to be balanced in front of any audience, and not to be shy or withdrawn."

One year at the state competition, the judges gave our team the maximum number of points possible for every category, and some of the judges jumped up and hugged the children afterwards. A judge remarked, "How orderly and presentable you are, how tight as a group. You are very supportive of each other, not just a show. Deeply felt. Your solution was very unusual."

Another judge, who has observed our students for the past several years, remarked to me once, "Your kids are just so perfect. I love them. It seems as if creativity is infused into the whole curriculum at Maharishi School." This is a perceptive observation that describes what many parents and teachers have noticed about Consciousness-Based education. "Meditation allows the students' creativity to flow freely," says mother Renée Sluser, whose son Zac won a total of five state championships in speech competitions and Odyssey of the Mind. "They are not inhibited to say creative things, and are connected to each other's thinking on a very deep level."

Coach Headlee has noticed that "students at other schools actually have to be taught creativity. Consciousness-Based education makes our students naturally creative." It is this natural growth of creative intelligence that is the key to all the successes enjoyed by Maharishi School students.

Zach Nichols

Zach Nichols, whose team won the world championship, understands this very clearly. He says, "Transcendental Meditation not only has improved my mind–body coordination but has also given me a clear mind so I can focus on whatever needs my attention. This is essential to winning competitions, and I believe this is what gives us our 'edge.'"

My experience is that this creative edge our students display has no limitations. It shines through in whatever they do, so it's no surprise to find that they also excel in the traditionally creative fields of art and photography.

Fine art and photography awards

As I wander through the corridors of the school, I often stop to admire the exhibitions of student art and photography adorning the walls. A freelance photographer, visiting the school on a shoot for a national magazine, couldn't believe the uniformly high quality of the students' work. "It could be the work of professionals," he observed.

Greg Thatcher, longtime art teacher at the school, has worked with students from a wide range of backgrounds. "It's almost like they are multitalented," he says, "because a high percentage of them display competence across the entire curriculum, from art to science."

The creativity displayed by the students in all areas of their lives finds concrete expression in the fine arts. Maharishi School students consistently win top honors at art and photography competitions, both in Iowa and on the national level.

Sharon Koelblinger

For three years in a row, Maharishi School students have won first place in the Congressional High School Art Contest, qualifying them to display their art in the House of Representatives in Washington, D.C. Sharon Koelblinger, who was inspired to pursue art following a class at Maharishi School, has won the competition twice—a rare honor and an indication of her creativity and talent. The first year she won with a pencil drawing. The second year she won with a collage, which again demonstrated a superb technique and original artistry. The winning pieces were displayed with others from around the country in the Tunnel Gallery that connects the United States House of

Representatives office buildings and the U.S. Capitol Building.

Because of the liveliness of the students, Mr. Thatcher likes to challenge their abilities and encourages them to tap deep within their consciousness for creative expression. "These kids are extraordinary," he says. "You have to have faith in yourself in order to deal with the unknown factors in artistic expression, such as what materials to use, how to use them, what happens if I do this, when to finish, etc. They learn to trust themselves. They know how to take an idea and make it real."

"I am amazed at the consistently high quality of work from the Maharishi School students. They seem to be in a league of their own."

Maharishi School students have also distinguished themselves in the field of photography, displaying a refined level of technical ability coupled with a creative and fresh approach to the subject. At the State Media Festival, hosted by the Iowa Educational Media Association in Council Bluffs, Maharishi School students regularly sweep the awards. The judges are qualified professional photographers who evaluate the techniques the students use with the camera and in the darkroom. They give points for the composition, clarity, power, creativity, and technical approach of the photograph. "I am amazed at the consistently high quality of work from the Maharishi School students. They seem to be in a league of their own," said one judge.

Our students have brought home numerous national and international honors, winning the International Student–Teacher Photo Competition, and receiving many top awards at the Texas A&M Photographic Society's Annual High School Shoot-Out.

Photography teacher Carolyn Waksman, who has guided the students to many awards, explains the secret of Maharishi School's success. "Our students are adaptable, receptive, and willing to try something new. They are creative beyond belief. I give the same assignment year after year, and I still see photographs that I've never seen before. The creativity comes from deep inside and flows effortlessly into their creative expression."

"Creative beyond belief" is a phrase that resonates with me, as I have experienced this time and again during my years at the school. The insights of these students come from deep inside. Impulses of creative intelligence are always spontaneously bubbling up, giving a vision of the world that is refreshingly original and insightful.

Poetic and literary accomplishments

This sense of wonder at how our students are blossoming in the arts is shared by Louise Maidment, who teaches poetry writing. She says, "It's the receptivity of the students—they know no boundaries, especially in the creative field. They easily learn about poetic devices, their retrieval memory is great, and they are able to apply figurative language. A number of Middle School students are even able to write poetry using rhyming couplets, which is usually very difficult at that age. Every year, I get poetry from the seventh graders that is astounding. They have the ability to transcend the surface value of objects and capture their essence."

The ability to observe, and to make deep connections between the self and the natural world, spontaneously grows with Consciousness-Based education. It certainly makes teaching these students very fulfilling, and naturally contributes to their success in poetry and writing.

> **Twelve-year-old Minca Borg won the national "A World Fit for Children" essay contest, topping entries from 6- to 18-year-olds from all over the country.**

Maharishi School students have won the Iowa Young Poet of the Year award and the Iowa Young Writer of the Year award. They have also won national honors. For example, 12-year-old Minca Borg won the national "A World Fit for Children" essay contest, topping entries from 6- to 18-year-olds from all over the country. Ron D. Kistler, president of Creative Educational Systems of East Brunswick, New Jersey, which sponsored the essay contest, said, "We received many entries from around the country. All showed that their young writers really care about the world in which we live and want passionately to see it change for the better so that it works for all of us. Minca's stood out among them as an essay of vision and compassion."

In her award-winning essay, Minca writes:

Minca Borg

I believe a world fit for children would be a world of peace, for peace is an environment in which love, joy and all good things can grow in us.

A world fit for children would be a world fit for every human being, for every human and every animal, for every plant and every body of water. In this enlightened world, peace and love would flow from the soul of every person, creating waves of everlasting peace and bliss. Every part of creation would feel fulfillment and rapidly evolve. Our planet would be an inner light of our universe, forever radiating heaven, for it would in fact be heaven on earth.

Everything on earth will flow in harmony. This means we shall live in nature as part of the ecosystem and enjoy the presence of even those small spiders whom many of us fear, for when there is such tranquil peace within and love overflows into the universe, there is no room for negativity.

This inner health will grow. Everybody will then be physically healthy, and because we as human beings have such overpowering impact on the earth, once we are in this enlightened state, we will have realized the world is as we are. In this inner purity, we shall want the air to be pure, not full of pollution. We will want the water to be fresh, for the forests, marshes, rainforests, mountains, grasslands, and beaches to be untarnished so that our fellow animals of this earth will have a natural existence, and we with them. We will no longer want to be rich in material for ourselves, but rich in inner qualities for our universe. . . .

This world fit for children is possible. When ideal education is put to use, it will radiate peace to the community, which, in turn, will affect other communities throughout the world. Thus, a world fit for children will be created by children. We each can make the world fit for ourselves, so let us begin. Let us create inner peace and balance, so we may spread this inner joy throughout the world. Thank you for helping to create a world fit for children.

Channing Swanson

History Fair success

It was no surprise for me to hear that Channing Swanson had won the State History Fair, placing first in the Individual Documentary category, because Channing has a way of fulfilling her aspirations. Her ten-minute video documentary entitled "Title IX: Turning Point for Women in Sports and Society" also won a cash award from the Iowa Federation of Women's Clubs in recognition of its contribution to the study of Women's History.

Janet Thomas, Channing's teacher, remarked that her achievement was the result of months of work and that "she applied herself to her research with great energy and enthusiasm, and she had to learn to master the completely unfamiliar medium of video documentary."

Channing has that same bright, cheerful quality I see in all our students, and she excels at everything she decides to do. "Meditation gives me so much energy and confidence that I feel I can achieve anything," Channing says.

Maharishi School students have captured five state titles in the senior division of the State History Fair and have gone on to represent Iowa at the National History Fair in Washington, D.C.

This success in History Fair doesn't come merely from learning and reciting facts and figures. It happens because Consciousness-Based education develops the same creative intelligence that has been displayed in the lives of great men and women throughout history.

At Maharishi School, we are developing the great leaders of the coming generation—individuals who will lead the way in all fields of knowledge, from mathematics to the arts to poetry and literature and the sciences as well.

Winning science competitions

Ted Wallace

Gareth Wallace

When Ted Wallace, son of Dr. Keith Wallace, the first scientist to publish research on the benefits of the Maharishi Transcendental Meditation program, won the State Science Fair in 1986, I thought it was perhaps beginner's luck. When his younger brother Gareth won in 1987 and came in third at the International Science Fair in Puerto Rico, I thought maybe it was a coincidence, or perhaps it was because their father is an accomplished scientist. But now that I have seen Maharishi School students win the senior division of state science fairs ten times, I am convinced that this success is due to Consciousness-Based education, which creates students who can succeed in whatever they set out to accomplish.

In the Junior Division of the Eastern Iowa Science and Engineering Fair, Maharishi School students have won eight grand champion awards in the past decade, impressing the judges with their maturity and grasp of abstract concepts.

One thing I have noticed about Maharishi School students is that when they are given the opportunity to apply their scientific knowledge, they naturally gravitate toward creating healthy solutions to the problems they see in society. For example, when they have entered the State Science Fair, their projects have included studies to investigate the cancer-prevention potential of herbal preparations, the creation of a new solution for photographic development to replace mercury with a less toxic alternative, and the invention of the alterbine, a turbine designed to generate pollution-free electricity from ocean currents.

Maharishi School students gravitate toward finding healthy solutions to the problems they see in society.

Science teacher Leslie Seal, who has seen two of her own children graduate from Maharishi School, says, "Judges often come up to me and ask questions about our students, noticing that they have the ability to 'think outside the box.' They also comment that our students are so confident within themselves that it's like talking to mature adults."

Jonathan Czinder, who, with his partner Daniel Blum, won State and came in fourth at the International Science and Engineering Fair, gives credit to Consciousness-Based education for his success. "It is so easy to come up with creative ideas spontaneously. It's like I do less and accomplish more."

Michelle Punj, who was a sophomore when she won first place in the senior division of the State Science Fair, showed that there was a flaw in the paper-backed insulation used to insulate hot pipes in power plants. The project found that the published emissivity rates were faulty, possibly making the insulation hazardous and putting people's lives at risk. When the insulation company heard of this project, they gave her other products to test. "I really enjoyed Science Fair this year," said Michelle. "It was really fulfilling to know that my research could make the workplace safer." As a senior, Michelle won the state singles tennis championship, but that is another story.

5

Skill in Action:
Enjoying Athletic Excellence

When I was in graduate school, I remember that in the lobby of the recreation center was a bronze bust depicting an athlete with his face contorted in pain. The inscription read "Effort Strain Fatigue." It did not look as if he was having much fun.

However, the philosophy of "no pain, no gain" seems to hold sway in the minds of many coaches and athletes today. A wrestling coach, who was an Olympic gold medalist, told me that when he was at school he worked out until he was unable to leave the gym without assistance. He said his proudest moment, other than receiving his gold medal, was when his high school daughter collapsed exhausted ten meters from the finish of the state 800-meter finals. He took this as a sign that she had given her best effort.

However, straining to exhaustion is not an efficient way to achieve success in life. If I want to move an arrow 100 yards to a target, I can either expend effort sprinting with the arrow and plunging it into the target, or I can do less and accomplish more by using the simple technique offered by a bow. This is skill in action. At Maharishi School our physical education and competitive sports programs adopt this principle of "do less and accomplish more" by using the techniques offered by Consciousness-Based education. Athletic activities are designed to develop exhilaration, creativity, and vitality in the students.

When Maharishi School won its first state tennis championship, a sports reporter wrote that TM stands for "Tennis Menace." This quote proved to be visionary, as the school has gone on to claim 17 state championships.

I have observed that Consciousness-Based education results in students who are not only healthier and more intelligent but also better coordinated. Put students with these qualities together with a great coach, and great athletes will naturally emerge.

"Tennis Menace"

When Maharishi School won its first state tennis championship in 1991, a sports reporter wrote that TM stands for "Tennis Menace." This quote proved to be visionary, as the school has gone on to claim 17 state championships since then and has become the first school in Iowa history to twice win the boys'

"Triple Crown" of singles, doubles, and team tennis in the same year.

Three-time state singles champion Tyler Cleveland, whom one opponent likened to playing a "pterodactyl in Nikes," says, "When you're on the court, there are so many distractions. Having the ability to focus: that's the crucial thing."

Tyler Cleveland

Tyler went on to be the number one player at the University of Iowa. During his undergraduate years, he was voted Freshman of the Year, Sportsman of the Year, and Big Ten player of the Year. Tyler has won both the Midwest Intercollegiate Championship and the Big Ten Singles Championship—the first Iowa player to accomplish this feat in over 40 years.

Tyler's opponents express amazement that he's grown up in this small town yet been so successful. As a teenager, Tyler led a balanced sports life, playing other sports as well as tennis. He was a starter on our varsity basketball team. "Nobody at this level even played another sport in high school," says his mother, Debbie. "It comes from deep inside of him, a feeling of self-sufficiency and inner strength." Tyler was subsequently voted Athlete of the Year at the University of Iowa, the first time a tennis player has ever won this honor.

Tyler always returns to watch the Maharishi School

sports teams (the "Pioneers") whenever he can. He has even seen his record of winning three state tennis championships equaled by another Pioneer, Naren Clark, who was only 11 when Cleveland brought home his first state championship.

Naren Clark

"He seemed so big, but I knew someday I could win it, too," Naren confessed. Little did he know that he would go on to win his first state singles championship while still a freshman.

Naren's final was dramatic against three-time state runner-up, senior Kurt Schuler from Red Oak. Clark raced to a 6-0 first-set win, but the more experienced Schuler took the second set 6-2. Then ensued a nail-biting third set with the match going to Naren in a tie-breaker. Naren's composure attracted the attention of the crowd. Several people remarked that they could not believe he was only a freshman—not because of his size and strength, nor because of his remarkable skill level, but because of his composure under fire. "He's so silent . . . he's so silent," one coach said, shaking his head.

Naren summed up his ability to stay cool under pressure in the following way: "The students at our school seem to play more from within themselves. Many times [at matches] you can see things get quite violent verbally—even in tennis it gets competitive and heated up. I am able to stay calm and focused on the match rather than letting my emotions carry me away."

Naren's victory led the Pioneers to their first Triple Crown. The following year, the team became the first in Iowa history to win the Triple Crown twice. The local *Fairfield Ledger* reported the team's achievements under the headline "Simply the Best," saying, "Someone will have to find a way to slip another boys' tennis trophy into the trophy case after Tuesday's brilliant performance. . . . The Pioneers didn't lose a match Tuesday, and their 16 [boys'] state championships overall since 1991 tie them with Camanche for the most in Iowa history. The Maharishi School, since it started its tennis program in 1988, is 151-37."

The team was also featured in an article in *Tennis Magazine* in April 2003. Maharishi School coach Lawrence Eyre, recently voted USTA Midwest Coach of the Year, is always being complimented and asked what the secret is to

his team's success. He says, "Our students are the ones who are able to integrate the skills and knowledge much more quickly and smoothly. I notice that their subtle mind–body coordination improves, giving them multifaceted creativity and stability amidst challenge. No doubt about it, TM is the key."

Michelle Punj

In recent years, our girls' tennis program has started to develop as well, winning the district championship for the past four years in a row and finishing third at state. Michelle Punj, the State Science Fair winner, also won the state singles championship in a three-set thriller that was tied 5–5 in the third set. Michelle says, "I feel quietly confident on the court. I am not angry. I don't get too emotional. Whatever happens, happens."

With sports becoming ever more competitive and demanding, I feel very fortunate that our students can enjoy success in competition without the negative side effects of strain, fatigue, and burnout. There is no doubt in my mind that the Transcendental Meditation program will become an indispensible part of the training regimen of most athletes in the years to come.

Track: Success without distress

I remember when Kevin Incorvia first took up running

the 800 meters when he was nine years old. Even then, it was clear that he had great potential as an athlete. Fortunately, he was able to develop his abilities without straining himself.

While many track coaches hold to the maxim "no pain, no gain," Kevin was fortunate to be trained by his coach to run while using only 50% of his maximum capacity. In this way, his growing nervous system was able to develop without creating stress and

Kevin Incorvia

tension in his life. His mind was not fatigued but clear and fresh, so he excelled academically at school. In his senior year, Kevin was determined to complete his high school career by reaching the state finals of the 800 meters. Kevin qualified for the finals by winning the district championship, and on the day of the state finals he was quietly confident. Because of the large number of competitors, the 800-meter final was run in two heats.

I watched Kevin's face as the winner of the first heat finished in a time which was faster than Kevin's personal best by over two seconds. He looked calm but said he wasn't sure if he could raise the bar by that much. However, he decided to run his own race, stayed with the pack on the first lap, and took the lead at the bell. I remember him pulling away from the rest of the field, and down the back stretch the announcer exclaimed, "Maharishi is in command!"

Kevin continued to pull away, taking 4.7 seconds off his personal best to set a new Class 1A state record. He described the race as "effortless" and didn't realize that this quantum leap in his performance had occurred. Vital, intelligent, and exhilarated, Kevin had gained without pain.

Golf: Accomplishment without anxiety

I enjoy watching our students play golf because golf is played in silence. Of course, for the player it can be stressful, and the appearance of outer calm may mask the inner nervousness agitating the player's mind. "You need inner silence to balance the dynamism of competition,"

> **"You need inner silence to balance the dynamism of competition."**

says Ted Hirsch, a member of the Maharishi School team that won the state championship. "Feeling settled inside makes you quietly confident, so it's easier to make a putt," says Noah Schechtman, another team member.

Maharishi School began its golf program in 1994 and finished third in the state finals that year. The following year, Lyric Duveyoung won the state individual championship, sinking a ten-footer for a birdie on the first hole of a play-off. The team finished as state runners-up.

In 1996 the team won the state championship, and after another five appearances at the state finals, Coach Ed Hipp was voted Coach of the Year 2003 by the Iowa High School Golf Coaches Association.

Sports Illustrated published a feature article on the team in December 1996, generating considerable interest within the golfing community. In fact, the article inspired a group of golf professionals to come to Fairfield to learn the Transcendental Meditation technique. After returning home and playing in a tournament, one pro wrote to us and said, "Meditation and calm carried the day!! This is the best I've ever felt. My mind was the clearest of any event to date."

Another golf pro enthused, "I'm more relaxed and clear-headed. I have more of a vision about my life and my golf." Yet another remarked, "I haven't missed one meditation. It changed my life. I absolutely love it. Nothing gets me cranked up and unglued like it used to. Stuff just rolls right off. I've never had more fun playing golf."

Noah Schechtman and Ted Hirsch are working with

their former coach Ed Hipp on the design and financing of an environmentally friendly golf course in Fairfield. "We want to be at the forefront of the organic revolution," says Noah. "Since we are deeply connected with our environment, the health of the whole community will benefit from the develop-ment of non-polluting agri-

> **"It is consciousness that connects our players and makes them play as one."**

cultural and recreational programs." These graduates of Maharishi School represent the thinking of a new genera-tion of Americans whose desire is to create a high quality of life in harmony with Natural Law.

Basketball: Unity in diversity

Watching Maharishi School students play basketball is fun. Everyone seems to keep in good perspective that it's just a game, and the joy comes from working together as a team. "We flourish on team coherence. It is con-sciousness that connects our players and makes them play as one," says coach Harley Carter.

Sofia Iwobi

Sofia Iwobi, who transferred from public school in grade seven and has since led the Lady Pioneers to two dis-trict championships, says, "Playing for Maharishi School is the best team experience ever. In public school I felt very insecure, but here it's OK to be different. Everyone's very supportive and unselfish—totally coherent. You won't find people like this anywhere else!"

This coherence applies not only to the players but also to the fans, whom referees consistently rate among the best in Iowa. "Referees enjoy it here," says Carter. "They appreciate the great facilities, but they also love the atmosphere."

When the boys' division title came down to the last game of the regular season, the Pioneers were playing away at the division leaders' court. The crowd was partisan, but the boys pulled off a great win. After the game, our opponents' school superintendent told me, "You have the most positive, energetic crowd we've seen here all year."

The boys went on to win their division of

> "The Substate game was without exception the finest display of sportsmanship by a non-winning side that I have ever witnessed. Congratulations!"

the Southeast Iowa Superconference with a 12-0 record and then went on to win the District Championship. At Substate they lost a close game to the eventual state champions, finishing the season with a 23-2 mark.

But it was the nature of the loss that impressed the fans. One supporter of the winning team wrote to the *Fairfield*

Ledger, "The Pioneer players, coaches, and fans deserve praise for their outstanding season and sportsmanship. Unfortunately, only one team may advance to state and therein lies a true test of character for the players, coaches, and spectators who do not prevail. The Maharishi School community certainly passed this test in exemplary fashion. I have watched dozens of basketball games over the years and have officiated high school football in Iowa for 10 years. The Substate game was without exception the finest display of sportsmanship by a non-winning side that I have ever witnessed. Congratulations! The Maharishi School players, coaches, and fans obviously know what sportsmanship is all about."

The equanimity and evenness that our students display, both in victory and defeat, is a sign of the growth of personal enlightenment and invincibility, where the ups and downs of everyday life do not overshadow the ever-present inner stability of the Self. This ability to exhibit skill in action without being thrown off balance by stressful situations has profound implications for health, as we shall see in the next chapter.

Maharishi School of the Age of Enlightenment
HIGHLIGHTS OF ACHIEVEMENTS

In the past decade, students at Maharishi School have won more than 100 state titles in science, speech, drama, writing, poetry, spelling, art, photography, history, mathematics, chess, tennis, golf, track, and Destination ImagiNation, a national and international creative problem-solving competition.

Grades 10–12 score in the top 1% nationally, and in Iowa, on standardized tests (ITED)

95% of graduates accepted at four-year colleges

Over ten times the nation's average for National Merit Scholar Finalists over the past five years

State Record: 41 state championships in creative problem-solving competitions Destination ImagiNation and Odyssey of the Mind

World Record: Three-time winners of the Global Finals of Destination ImagiNation, and more top-ten finishes than any other school in the world

First Place: American High School Math Exam, Iowa Division, four years in a row

First Place: Five first-place finishes, Iowa State History Fair, Senior Division

First Place: Ten first-place finishes in the senior division of the Eastern Iowa or Hawkeye state science fairs

Grand Champions: Eight grand champion awards in the past decade in the junior division of the Eastern Iowa Science and Engineering Fair

First place: Twice winner of the state spelling bee

State Record: Most Critic's Choice State Banner Awards for speech in the past decade

National Champion: Bravo Cable Channel High School Theater Competition

State Record: Congressional Art Competition, "An Artistic Discovery," grand prize three years in a row

First Place: Iowa Poetry Association's high school contest

First Place: Iowa "Young Writer of the Year" award

State Champion: Iowa Junior Chess Championship

First Place: Iowa Educational Media Association (Photography)

Grand Prize: International Photo Imaging Education Association competition

State Champions: 16 boys' state tennis championships, tying for the most in Iowa history

State Champion: Girls' state singles tennis

State Record: Tennis Triple Crown winner two years in a row

State Record: Boys' track 800 meters

State Champions: Golf team and individual

6

Averting the Danger:
Preventing Health Problems
in This Generation

I remember giving a lecture on the health benefits of the Transcendental Meditation technique to a group of doctors at a teaching hospital in Montreal back in the 1970s. The chief resident told me, "I enjoyed your presentation, but you are wasting your time talking to doctors. They aren't interested in health; they're interested in disease."

The chief resident went on to say that time was so limited in medical school that they didn't even have time to wade through all the diseases, so where would they find time for an additional course on prevention? This seemed to me to be like the captain of a sinking ship saying that his crew members are so busy bailing out the water that they don't have time to fix the leak. Fortunately, today the emphasis in health care is shifting toward prevention, and Maharishi School is leading the way with the coming generation by training students not only to prevent disease but also to promote ideal health.

The term *health care* today is really a euphemism for

disease care. Although the U.S. spends much more on health care than other industrialized countries, almost 100 million Americans suffer from chronic diseases, such as hypertension, for which modern medicine has no cure, according to a study published in the *Journal of the American Medical Association*.[18]

Chronic diseases account for over three-quarters of all direct medical costs—a highly significant finding given that annual health-care costs in America are forecast to exceed $2 trillion by 2007.[19] Health professionals estimate that a high percentage of disease results from chronic stress[20,21] and that up to 90% of all visits to primary care physicians are for stress-related problems.[22]

Current education offers little to combat stress and to promote good health in the nation's youth. The outcome is that stress-related disorders such as obesity, diabetes, hypertension, and anxiety are on the rise among young people, threatening to shorten their life expectancy significantly. Indeed, doctors have a growing fear that many children today may not outlive their parents.

Since the majority of stress-related ailments are preventable, the prevention-oriented health education programs offered at Maharishi School not only prevent many of these diseases but also offer the only viable solution to the problem of spiraling health-care costs.

Preventing cardiovascular disease

I was delighted the other day when the local nurse, during her annual visit to give the children their sports physicals, dropped by my office and said, "I've noticed your students have lower blood pressure than the students at the other schools in the area."

Interestingly, I had just spoken with Dr. Vernon Barnes, a physiologist at the Medical College of Georgia's Prevention Institute in Augusta about a study he and his co-workers had just published in the *American Journal of Hypertension*.[23] He told me that in this study of 156 African-American adolescents with high-normal blood pressure, "Teens who practiced 15 minutes of the Transcendental Meditation program twice daily lowered their daytime

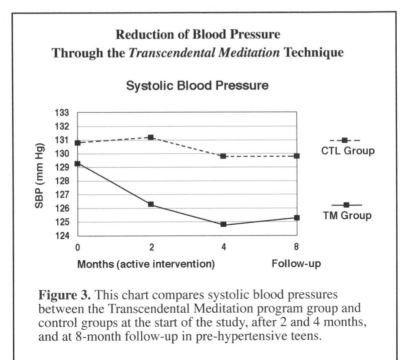

Figure 3. This chart compares systolic blood pressures between the Transcendental Meditation program group and control groups at the start of the study, after 2 and 4 months, and at 8-month follow-up in pre-hypertensive teens.

Reference: 23

blood pressures over four months, and their pressures tended to stay lower." (See Figure 3.) This normalization of blood pressure occurred without harmful side effects—only side benefits, such as significant reductions in absenteeism, rule infractions, and suspension rates at school.[24]

It is well known that stress contributes to many health problems, such as high blood pressure and cardiovascular disease, but it can also lead to behavior problems. So I wasn't surprised to learn that the Transcendental Meditation program reduced stress-related disorders and also led to improvements in behavior.

Since cardiovascular disease is the leading cause of death in America today, and misbehavior is plaguing our schools and communities, these findings are of crucial significance to educators who want to prevent future problems in the lives of their students.

Pioneering prevention

Research on the Transcendental Meditation technique has led to a growing recognition by the government and the medical community that many common diseases can be prevented.

The National Institutes of Health and a number of private foundations have awarded over $18 million in research grants to Maharishi University of Management's Institute of Natural Medicine and Prevention. Medical researchers at the Institute led by Dr. Robert Schneider, together with collaborators from 12 leading U.S. universities and research institutes, have found that the Transcendental Meditation program reduces cardiovascular disease and morbidity and is the most effective non-pharmacological method of normalizing blood pressure.[25, 26]

> **The Transcendental Meditation program is the most effective non-pharmacological method of normalizing blood pressure.**

A healthy school community

At a recent meeting of local high school administrators, I had a discussion about health insurance costs with a superintendent whose school has about the same number of faculty as we do. I learned that the cost of his school's health insurance program is over twice that of ours. In addition, his plan doesn't cover faculty dependents, so our cost per individual is actually about a quarter of his.

Again, I suppose this shouldn't have surprised me, because a study in *Psychosomatic Medicine*[27] had reported that the faculty at Maharishi School and at Maharishi University of Management were 50% less likely to be admitted to a hospital as compared with a control group. Furthermore, a study published in the *American Journal of Managed Care*[28] showed that individuals over the age of 45 who practiced the Transcendental Meditation technique and related programs had 88% fewer total patient days than matched controls.

Imagine the impact on our society as more and more children and adults are taught the simple, health-promoting technologies included in Consciousness-Based education! The savings, both in human suffering and in health-care costs, will be incalculable.

Education for prevention and promotion

Since the majority of stress-related ailments are preventable, it makes sense to make education "prevention oriented." At Maharishi School, starting in first grade, students take prevention-oriented health classes, which include simple techniques to promote good health and prevent disease. The goal is to "avert the danger that has not yet come." Topics include the importance of regular practice of the Transcendental Meditation program, healthy diet, prevention-oriented natural medicines, and the value of following daily and seasonal routines.

These programs, together with a balanced exercise program, promote a healthy mind in a healthy body. The result, for both students and faculty, is not merely prevention of disease but a vibrant wholesomeness that radiates into the environment, leaving the atmosphere in the school uniquely blissful.

Benefits for teachers: No more burnout

One striking benefit of having healthy students and teachers is that I do not encounter the problems with teacher burnout that afflict other schools. Says high school teacher Janet Thomas, "You can go into a classroom with any set of ideas, but often the situation changes according to differing student needs. I can adapt more easily now, and this has made me a much better teacher."

Fifth-grade teacher Gail Lynch, who has taught at the Maharishi School for almost 20 years and is well known for her challenging but fun science classes, says, "I couldn't imagine anything better than Consciousness-Based education in schools because it brings so many benefits. Even just the deep rest is a gold mine—and being able to tap my own inner resources of creativity is invaluable. I have a happy and hopeful feeling after meditating, with greater evenness during the day."

As an administrator, I have noticed how easy it is to work with our teachers. They are open to new ideas and can "turn on a dime" to implement them. "Personally, I think TM makes you more flexible," says Ms. Lynch. "Meditating allows your awareness to expand naturally. It is almost like you have blinders on before you learn to meditate, and once they're gone, you can expand your territory of influence, your horizons, and yourself."

These teachers are role models who motivate students to learn by their own example. Fortunately, as we will see in the next chapter, the excellence and wholesome atmosphere enjoyed by Maharishi School students and faculty can easily be achieved at any school, simply by incorporating Consciousness-Based education into the curriculum.

Above: First grader Nathaniel Zhu, enjoying a story with his class-mates. Below: Students in Maharishi School's award-winning theater arts program perform a choral reading.

Above: Upper School students Coral and Melodia Morales prepare for the state tennis finals. Below: Science Fair winners Daniel Blum and Jonathan Czinder look forward to the International Science Fair.

Above: National Merit Scholar Finalists (left to right): Amy Hart, Sarah Neate, Nicole Windenberger, Caitlin Allen. Below: Fifth-grade teacher Rena Boone, who has taught at Maharishi School for 25 years, shares a moment with Angelia Mahaney.

Above: Jon Hathaway in the senior class. Below: Freshman Cooper Rose practicing the Transcendental Meditation technique.

Above: Maharishi School Pioneers basketball team makes a basket. Below: Students at the Nataki Talibah Schoolhouse in Detroit practicing the Transcendental Meditation technique.

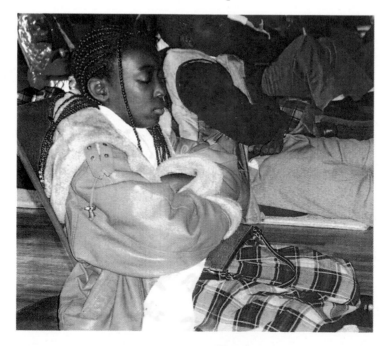

Above: First grader Sophia Goodale pays close attention to her teacher. Below: Dr. Vernon Barnes of the Medical College of Georgia's Prevention Institute, with some of the participants in his teenage hypertension study.

Above: The sign outside Maharishi School tells the tale of the students' achievements. Below: Coach Mark Headlee (front row, left) and the author (front row, right) with Odyssey of the Mind and Destination ImagiNation competition winners and their trophies.

7

Consciousness-Based Education in Schools

Principals often ask me, "Will I see immediate results if I intro-duce the Transcendental Meditation program into my school?" The answer is yes. And the benefits are noticeable immediately. That is not just my opinion; it is the experience at hundreds of schools, colleges, and universities around the world, with students representing a broad spectrum of economic, cultural, and religious backgrounds. Institutions as diverse as a middle school in Detroit, a university in Beijing, and a vocational college in South Africa are reporting unprecedented successes. In this chapter I offer results from a variety of schools in the United States.

Lower stress in Detroit, Michigan

In downtown Detroit, Michigan is the Nataki Talibah Schoolhouse, a charter school founded in 1978 by principal Carmen N'Namdi. With the aid of nearly $200,000 in grants from the DaimlerChrysler Foundation and the General Motors Corporation, she introduced the Transcendental Meditation program at Nataki in 1997.

Today over 100 students now meet twice daily in the school's auditorium for their group meditations.

Says Ms. N'Namdi, "To see that 10- and 11-year-old boys know the meaning of 'quiet' is amazing. So many people don't. And to see them sit quietly and meditate is incredible. The Transcendental Meditation program allows them to grow from a real experience, not from superficial things."

> **"To see 10- and 11-year-old boys sit quietly and meditate is incredible."**

In June 1999, an article in the *Detroit News* reported, "The Nataki Talibah Schoolhouse works the way champions of charter schools envisioned they should work." Since then, the school has enjoyed continuing success and currently has a lengthy waiting list for new students. "We want to help children manage their lives, and the Transcendental Meditation technique is a tool to get to the real self. Students are focusing better in class, and the whole school is more harmonious," says Ms. N'Namdi.

A research team led by Dr. Rita Benn, education researcher and director of the Education Department of the Center for Complementary and Alternative Medicine at the University of Michigan, found in a randomized pilot control study that the meditating children showed "significantly more positive emotions and positive mood state and greater emotional adaptability than non-meditating peers."

Dr. Benn's earlier research on the meditating school-children at Nataki found higher self-esteem, more positive well-being, improved management of stress and interpersonal skills, and less verbal aggression, anxiety, and loneliness. Says Dr. Benn, "If meditation has the capacity to facilitate kids feeling better about themselves, it has huge implications for other areas of their lives. It may prevent mental health difficulties—and it may reduce the likelihood of the need for medication."

The teachers also meditate together before and after school so that they can benefit from less stress. Says Ms. N'Namdi to her teachers, "I want to interact with you, not your stress. I want you to interact with your students, not your stress or their stress. I want us to get to the real people."

This experience in Detroit is typical of experiences with Consciousness-Based education in schools around the world. With students and faculty less stressed, greater harmony and mutual respect spontaneously develop, and incidents of bullying and violence decrease. Classes become more settled and corridors less chaotic. Teachers experience the joy of walking into a classroom where the students are developing their full mental potential, fully awake, eager, and ready to learn.

Improved learning in Silver Spring, Maryland

Chelsea School in Silver Spring, Maryland, just outside Washington, D.C., is a school for students with language-based learning disabilities. It is the site of a pioneering study on the use of the Transcendental Meditation program to combat attention deficit–hyperactivity disorder (ADHD)—the most common behavioral and psychiatric disorder among children.

"ADHD can cause a lifetime of frustration and emotional pain," says project director Dr. Sarina Grosswald of the Institute of Community Enrichment in Silver Spring. "The behavior of an ADHD child can create chaos in the classroom and in the home, causing stress and turmoil for the family and the school. Our research suggests TM is an excellent means to break that cycle."

As many as two million children suffer from ADHD, which can cause problems with concentration, self-control, memory, and overactivity—significantly impairing a child's ability to learn and progress in school. "We are studying the effectiveness of Transcendental Meditation as a behavioral intervention because there is already a large body of scientific research demonstrating the effectiveness of the technique on school performance, IQ, and problem solving," says Dr. William Stixrud, a prominent cognitive psychologist and co-researcher of the study.

Many of the children in the Chelsea School study take drugs like Ritalin, a widely prescribed amphetamine. Unfortunately, these drugs have been found to have numerous side effects, including decreased appetite, weight loss, reduced body growth, insomnia, nausea, headache, irritability and moodiness, and motor tics. Children taking these drugs have also been found to have a higher risk of substance abuse.

Consciousness-Based education promises to improve the children's learning ability without harmful side effects. "We are excited about the project," says Dr. Linda Handy, Chelsea School's academic director. "Our focus is our children, and any resource that can help these students, who struggle every day with their learning differences, is worthy of our involvement. Transcendental Meditation provides a powerful tool that belongs to our students, so they don't feel so alone in their struggle with ADHD. It is such a simple technique, and it doesn't interfere with any other treatment approach or personal beliefs. We feel it is a compassionate approach for helping our children."

> **"Transcendental Meditation provides a powerful tool that belongs to our students, so they don't feel so alone in their struggle with ADHD."**

Quiet time in Washington, D.C.

Dr. George Rutherford, an educator and public high school principal in Washington, D.C. for over 35 years, implemented Consciousness-Based education in his school, The Fletcher Johnson Educational Center, where he was

Dr. George
Rutherford

experiencing a wide range of problems. The benefits that ensued were so dramatic that I asked Dr. Rutherford to tell the story in his own words:

It was in 1989 that the problem of drugs in Washington, D.C. went big time. Young people started killing each other off. Washington became the number one murder city in the country—we averaged over 500 murders a year for four or five years.

I was concerned because a lot of violence was taking place right around my school, and many of my students were affected. We were in southeast Washington, D.C., recognized as the most dangerous area in the District. To get to school, my children had to walk between two housing projects, and rival gangs would shoot at each other, sometimes hitting my kids. I was out there trying to stop the fighting and to keep my kids safe. But I still had kids die in my arms. It was not an experience I wanted to go through ever again.

In 1992, one of my former students was convicted for murder and sent to the electric chair. Another one of my former students received 16 years to life because he shot at one person, missed, and hit a grandmother who was in the backyard playing with her granddaughter.

I realized that I had to do something to try to help these young people. It was at this time I had the opportunity to meet Dr. John Hagelin, a famous physicist and an expert on Transcendental Meditation. He came to my school and talked to my students. I wanted to know more about Transcendental Meditation, so I decided to learn the technique.

The TM Center was in Tacoma Park. I was uneasy because I didn't know what was going to happen. Once I got instructed, I felt so silly because it was such a pleasure to meditate. It was the greatest thing that ever happened to me. I felt so good.

At that point I told my wife of 35 years that she just had to learn it because she had a problem with hypertension. She was a little apprehensive because she is a devoutly religious person and thought it might be a conflict with her Christian belief. I assured her that it wouldn't. It was important that I got my wife meditating. She had five sisters—none of whom lived to be 55. All of them died from the same thing, and her mother too—aneurysm.

After my wife learned, she realized it had nothing to do with religion, and she encouraged our four children to learn also. It was a beautiful experience. It is very lovely when you have your whole family meditating.

It's been a great experience for me. I am healthier. I am able to do more in the school, and I am not as hyper as I used to be. The teachers recognized this and said, "Hey, Doc, whatever you're doing, we want some of that, too."

Gradually, over 150 students and 85% of my staff learned the Transcendental Meditation program. So that they could meditate together, we introduced what we call "quiet time." In the morning, from 8:50 a.m. to 9:10 a.m., was quiet time. Everyone in the school got quiet. Not all the students learned Transcendental Meditation, but all participated in "quiet time." Those who didn't practice just sat quietly or read a book or something. But we saw the stress level in the school come way down.

After quiet time, we found that we did not have any more fights during the mornings. The "fussing" students went to classes and got involved immediately in their schoolwork.

> **I noticed that the fighting stopped, not just with my kids inside the school, but outside in the street!"**

In the afternoon, from 3:10 p.m. to 3:30 p.m., we had "quiet time" again. I noticed that the fighting in the afternoon stopped, not just with my kids inside the school but outside in the street! I wasn't going around breaking up fights any more. Then our test scores started going up, attendance improved, and my teachers felt better. This was the greatest thing that could have happened to our school.

A few times folks questioned what I was doing. But I just did what I thought could make life better for someone else or for our whole community.

When you have something so valuable for young people, you've got to step up to the plate. We can sit in our homes and we can look at the news, and we can feel so sorry for those kids. But until we step forward, we have done nothing. Students in the inner city deserve to have a better quality of life just like the rest of us. Why should they have to be afraid of a drive-by shooting? Why shouldn't they be able to go home and sleep, study, get up, and come to school, without fear of anyone bothering them? Shouldn't they have the same opportunity as the rest of us?

"Students in the inner city deserve to have a better quality of life just like the rest of us."

I retired in 1998 after 35 years in the Washington, D.C. public school system, but I couldn't just stop this exciting work. Now we are starting again in the Ideal Academy, our D.C. charter school. We already have many teachers meditating, and the students will learn next. We want to keep the children alive. We want to raise academic achievement. We want to change the quality of life. That's all any of us want—a good quality of life for everyone—and I've seen how the Transcendental Meditation program can bring this about.

Preventing school violence

Dr. Rutherford's experience confirms what other educators around the world have found: Consciousness-Based education raises test scores, improves health, reduces individual and social stress, and creates a more harmonious school climate.

How can something so simple have such profound benefits? Maharishi Mahesh Yogi, the founder of the Transcendental Meditation program, has used the analogy of watering the root of a tree; this simple procedure nourishes the leaves, fruits, and branches because it enlivens their common source—the sap. Like that, the Transcendental Meditation program enlivens the field of creative intelligence within, leading to increased creativity, reduced stress, and more harmonious social behavior.

It's clear from 50 years of experience and hundreds of scientific research studies that the application of this knowledge offers a solution to some of the most critical problems of our age. The upsurge of fear and violence that is gripping many of America's schools is a clear indication that something is terribly wrong with our educational system. Harassment,

Rama Hall

bullying, and violence afflict many school communities. Security systems, metal detectors, and police patrols have become commonplace. However, none of these approaches has succeeded in neutralizing the rising stress levels that lead to antisocial behavior.

In contrast, Consciousness-Based education has proven successful. Maharishi School junior Rama Hall addressed the issue of school violence at a conference at the United Nations, organized by the Gandhi-King Foundation. He said, "We are offering students a solution to school violence and other stress-related problems that kids face.

Students have been groping in the dark far too long, and fortunately Transcendental Meditation has come along with a solution to turn the light on for them."

The decreased violence Dr. Rutherford observed in his school and in the surrounding community is not an isolated occurrence. It is a phenomenon that has been seen in many schools and communities, and is consistent with the findings of a large body of research.

One percent of a population practicing the Transcendental Meditation technique is sufficient to defuse acute social stress.

We have seen that the Transcendental Meditation technique reduces stress on the individual level, but how does this affect society as a whole? When we consider society as a collection of individuals, we can understand that even if just a few of the individuals are less stressed, the society as a whole will have less stress.

In 1960, Maharishi predicted that problems in society would decrease when just a few people had learned his Transcendental Meditation technique. Several studies have since confirmed that just one percent of a population practicing the Transcendental Meditation technique is sufficient to defuse acute social stress, as evidenced by reductions in negative trends such as crime and violence.[29, 30] This phenomenon is now known as the *Maharishi Effect*.

Reducing social stress

How can a small number of people practicing the Transcendental Meditation technique be sufficient to reduce violence in the society as a whole?

At first glance, the answer is not obvious. For example, the students at Dr. Rutherford's school (see pages 101–105) did not go out into their neighborhood and try to decrease the violence; they simply sat and practiced the Transcendental Meditation program for a few minutes twice a day in school.

But we have seen that this simple technique reduces stress in the individual and increases the coherent functioning of the brain. Could it be that Dr. Rutherford's students were reducing stress and increasing coherence in the whole community? According to modern science, this is possible. Here's how.

Field effects

We all learned in school that the earth moves around the sun by virtue of the force of gravity. According to physics, it is the gravitational *field* that allows the sun to influence the earth from a distance. We also learned about the magnetic field, which can act on a compass needle thousands of miles from the earth's magnetic poles.

Today, we take such invisible fields for granted. But this wasn't always the case. For example, in 1901 a board appointed by the U.S. Navy recommended the adoption of the radio to send information via the electromagnetic field, but the top brass continued to invest resources in homing pigeons for over 40 years.[31] Presumably, the concept of utilizing invisible fields was too abstract for them to fully accept.

Creating coherence

One remarkable property of fields is that harmonious or coherent collective functioning can be established throughout a system through a principle called the *field effect*. For example, consider the powerful properties of coherent light from a laser.

Why is laser light more coherent than the random, disorderly light emitted by the atoms in a fluorescent bulb? Because in a laser, coherent light from a few atoms enlivens the electromagnetic field, resulting in a field effect that stimulates the rest of the atoms to radiate coherently as well. This sudden shift from incoherent to coherent collective behavior is an example of a *phase transition.*

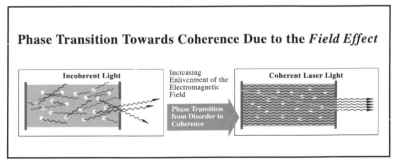

Phase Transition Towards Coherence Due to the *Field Effect*

Incoherent Light

Increasing Enlivenment of the Electromagnetic Field

Phase Transition from Disorder to Coherence

Coherent Laser Light

We will now consider how a similar phase transition from incoherence to coherence can be produced in society by just a few people practicing the Transcendental Meditation technique.

The Unified Field

How could a phase transition from incoherence to coherence occur in society? And what field could be involved? Just as the branches, leaves, and fruits of a tree are all expressions of one underlying sap, modern physics reveals that at the most fundamental level of nature's functioning all the diverse force and particle fields in the universe spring from a common source—the Unified Field. (See Figure 4.)

If everything in the universe is an expression of one Unified Field, then fundamentally, at our core, all of us are connected with everyone and everything. The Unified Field is the unified source of knower, process of knowing, and known. It is the unified fountainhead of all streams of knowledge—physics, chemistry, art, economics, etc. It is a field of Total Knowledge and infinite organizing power.

Consciousness and the Unified Field

Let's look more closely at the nature of the Unified Field, which is the core of our existence. The Unified Field is self-interacting—in other words, it is self-referral; it creates from within itself by referring to itself alone. But self-referral, or self-awareness, is the characteristic quality of consciousness! This realization leads to the understanding that the essential nature of the Unified Field of modern physics

> The essential nature of the Unified Field of modern physics is consciousness —the core of our existence.

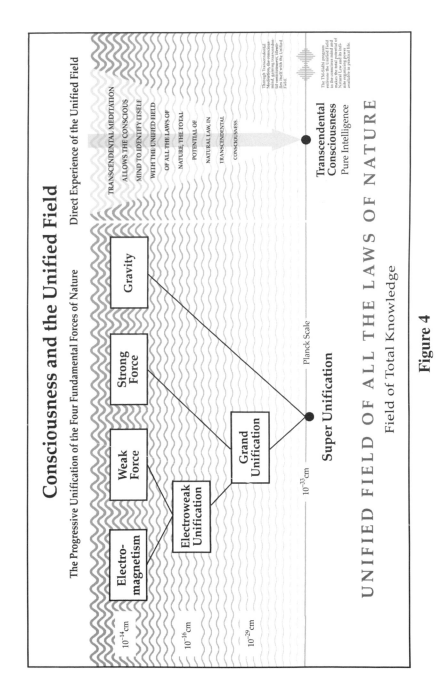

Figure 4

is consciousness[32]—the core of our existence—the Self of every individual.

This provides insight into the field effect by which a small group of individuals enlivening the Unified Field—the field of consciousness—through the Transcendental Meditation technique spontaneously generates an influence of harmony and coherence in the whole society, giving rise to the Maharishi Effect.

Phase Transition Towards Coherence Due to the Maharishi Effect

Increasing Enlivenment of the Field of Consciousness Due to the Group Practice of the Transcendental Meditation and TM-Sidhi Programs, Including Yogic Flying

Phase Transition from Disorder to Coherence

Incoherent Society

Coherent Society

In the following chapter we shall see that, through the group practice of the Transcendental Meditation technique and the advanced TM–Sidhi® program, which includes a simple, effortless technique known as Yogic Flying, the Maharishi Effect can be produced even more powerfully in a very practical manner to prevent violence on a global scale.

8

Preventing Violence
on a Global Scale

When Dr. George Rutherford first visited Maharishi School in 1991, I was saddened to hear of the problems he was facing every day. The fact that he persisted in his attempts to help his children under such difficult circumstances told me a lot about his character. I was pleased when he told me that he was going to return to D.C. and implement Consciousness-Based education in his own school. His success story shows that anyone, anywhere, can implement this program in a school and reduce social stress in the local community. But violence is not just a problem in our schools—it tears apart societies and nations as a whole. Could the Transcendental Meditation technique and its advanced programs be applied to address this larger problem as well?

To reduce violence on a global scale through the Transcendental Meditation technique alone would, according to research, require one percent of the world's population. This would involve over 60 million people worldwide, including three million Americans. While teaching this many people could easily be done in principle, it would obviously take some time in practice.

However, over 40 research projects[33-44] have demonstrated that the group practice of Transcendental Meditation and the advanced TM-Sidhi program, including Yogic Flying, reduces social stress even more powerfully than the Transcendental Meditation technique alone. Yogic Flying, where the body lifts up and moves forward in a series of short hops, demonstrates the ability to engage the total creative potential of Natural Law in Transcendental Consciousness, at the junction point of consciousness and physiology. This is the level of Super Unification where gravity emerges from the Unified Field. (See Figure 4.)

The body lifting up indicates the success of the Yogic Flying program and demonstrates access to the creativity of the Unified Field—the self-referral state of consciousness. The body lifts up at the point of maximum coherence in brain wave activity, while the Yogic Flyer enjoys bubbling bliss. Groups of Yogic Flying students will radiate coherence and harmony to their community and nation.

Research shows that during Yogic Flying the body lifts up at the point of maximum brain wave coherence[45,46] (see Figure 5), generating a powerful influence of harmony and positivity in the collective consciousness of society.

While these concepts may be new to the reader, research on Yogic Flying and the Maharishi Effect has been published in the most prestigious, peer-reviewed academic

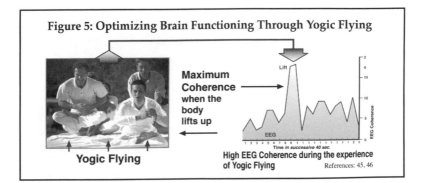

Figure 5: Optimizing Brain Functioning Through Yogic Flying

Maximum Coherence when the body lifts up

Yogic Flying

High EEG Coherence during the experience of Yogic Flying   References: 45, 46

journals. A case in point: a study in the *Journal of Conflict Resolution*,[36] published by Yale University Press, showed a significant reduction of violence in war-torn areas when the size of the group exceeded just the square root of one percent of the population.

Creating groups of Yogic Flyers provides a practical approach to reducing violence on a national and global scale, because for a world population of 6.4 billion, the square root of one percent is only 8,000 people. So in

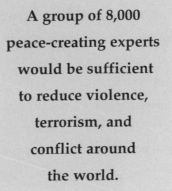

A group of 8,000 peace-creating experts would be sufficient to reduce violence, terrorism, and conflict around the world.

summary, according to published research, a group of 8,000 peace-creating experts would be sufficient to reduce violence, terrorism, and conflict around the world.

Students creating peace

It is remarkable that a small group of people, such as students in a school, can reduce stress, violence, and conflict in a whole society. This is possible because Consciousness-Based education provides the student with the ability to think and act from the most fundamental level of consciousness—the Unified Field—at the source of thought. This culminating discovery of modern science heralds a new era where schools will radiate positivity and coherence for the whole society.

And because it is so enjoyable, Yogic Flying is very popular with students. At Maharishi School and Maharishi University of Management, students from all religions and backgrounds blissfully practice this ancient technique both for the development of their own consciousness and to help create world peace.

Maharishi School senior Geoff Boothby says, "Yogic Flying is one of the highlights of my day. I always look forward to it. When I lift off, my body feels as light as air. I feel deeply blissful and happy inside. It's so easy, too—like Transcendental Meditation, the whole thing is automatic."

With the rising threat of terrorism and weapons of mass destruction in the world today, America urgently needs groups of Yogic Flyers. These groups can be composed of students attending public or private schools and can be publicly or privately funded. The students can participate in Yogic Flying Clubs as an extracurricular activity—with the byproduct of creating peace in the world. And the cost is entirely practical, too. For just a fraction of the cost of one B2 bomber, a school district could be permanently endowed to maintain such a group.

Creating groups of Yogic Flyers is the only practical way

to bring invincibility to the nation—to prevent violence or negativity arising within the country or entering the country from outside. With groups of Yogic Flyers established at many schools throughout the nation, national consciousness will become highly coherent, filled with peace and harmony. Enmity against the nation will turn to friendship, and the nation will enjoy invincibility—prevention of the birth of any enemies. (See Figure 6.)

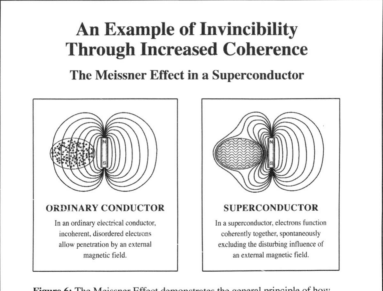

An Example of Invincibility Through Increased Coherence

The Meissner Effect in a Superconductor

ORDINARY CONDUCTOR

In an ordinary electrical conductor, incoherent, disordered electrons allow penetration by an external magnetic field.

SUPERCONDUCTOR

In a superconductor, electrons function coherently together, spontaneously excluding the disturbing influence of an external magnetic field.

Figure 6: The Meissner Effect demonstrates the general principle of how coherent functioning of a system results in the ability to defend against external disturbing influences.

This example of invincibility is not unique in nature: parallel phenomena of invincibility or indestructibility may be found in many aspects of the physical and biological sciences. In each case, we find that a situation of invincibility is always based on coherence of collective functioning.

Invincibility on the level of society can be achieved through the Maharishi Effect, whereby coherence in collective consciousness is created and maintained through the group practice of the Transcendental Meditation and TM-Sidhi program, including Yogic Flying.

In this age of nuclear terrorism, it is the urgent need of our time for educators in both the public and private sectors to take their cue from pioneers such as Dr. Rutherford and help to implement the Transcendental Meditation and TM–Sidhi program, including Yogic Flying, into schools and colleges everywhere to bring invincibility to the nation before it is too late.

Nelina Loiselle

Maharishi School student Nelina Loiselle, a founding member of the Students Creating Peace Network, understands the power of this peace-creating technology for the coming generations: "When Consciousness-Based education is offered in every school, the world will be so much better. There won't be all this violence and negativity. To create peace, we have to start with our Self. It takes peaceful individuals to make a peaceful world. Consciousness-Based education allows us to have that time to settle down, to go within to experience our own Self—the field of perfect peace—and create the effect of peace from there."

9

Introducing *Consciousness-Based* Education into a School

I cannot think of anything more satisfying for an educator than to have the opportunity to work with students who are healthy, wide awake, creative, and enthusiastic—who are enjoying the benefits of Consciousness-Based education. Visitors to Maharishi School often tell me that I am sitting on the best-kept secret in the world. I hope this book changes that situation and inspires educators and parents to introduce Consciousness-Based education into schools in their communities.

How to start this program in your school

By now you may be asking, "How can I introduce Consciousness-Based education into my local school?" It is hard to think of anything easier. Simply introduce a few minutes of "quiet time" at the start and end of the school day when students can practice their Transcendental Meditation program. And that's it!

Indeed, the only difficult thing about Consciousness-

Based education is understanding how easy it is to implement. Any school can start the program because no new equipment or facilities are needed. Students just sit comfortably and meditate in their classrooms, or in an assembly hall or gymnasium, and the benefits are seen immediately. Dr. George Rutherford

> **The only difficult thing about Consciousness-Based education is understanding how easy it is to implement.**

reported, "As soon as we started the TM program, we could see the changes. Our school became one of the best schools in Washington, D.C. To walk in and feel the sweetness in the air was such a good feeling. Children would stop and speak to any visitor in the school and would do anything to help anyone. It was beautiful."

Learning the Transcendental Meditation technique

Personal instruction in the Transcendental Meditation program occurs in seven steps, which can be arranged at the convenience of parents and school administrators. Because everyone is unique, the technique cannot be learned from a book; it has to be taught by a trained teacher. Appendix III provides the information you will need to contact the Consciousness-Based Education Association (CBEA), which can arrange to get a program started in a school, including instruction in the Transcendental Meditation technique and the follow-up program of knowledge for teachers and students. If you would like to learn the Transcendental Meditation technique yourself, Appendix III provides the information about how to contact a qualified teacher in your local area.

In addition to offering Consciousness-Based education in existing public and private schools, Maharishi Peace Palaces* are being constructed in the 3,000 largest cities of the world. These Peace Palaces will be centers of knowledge that teach the Transcendental Meditation program, its advanced techniques, and the TM-Sidhi program, including Yogic Flying. They will include a Maharishi Spa offering Maharishi Ayur-Veda^{SM} prevention-oriented health programs and herbal preparations, Maharishi Vedic^{TM} organic agriculture, and Maharishi Jyotish^{SM} (Vedic Astrology) and Maharishi Yagya^{SM} programs, to help prevent future health problems. The Peace Palaces will include Consciousness-Based schools and universities, which will give brain integration report cards to measure the growth of total brain functioning as students rise to enlightenment.

---

*Maharishi Peace Palaces are built according to the architectural principles of Maharishi Sthapatya Veda^{SM} design—the Vedic knowledge of building in accord with Natural Law. These Peace Palaces will be the pride of their communities. They will serve as the Capitals of the Global Country of World Peace, a country without borders founded to provide a home for peace-loving people everywhere. For information on how to invest in a Peace Palace in your area, visit www.globalcountry.org.

10

New Principles of Education Resulting from the Experience of Total Knowledge

Adding Consciousness-Based education to the school curriculum is very simple, yet the results are profound. Sometimes I wonder what would happen if a simple technique were discovered that prevented the harmful effects of stress—a causal factor in 90% of all diseases. I imagine it would be hailed as the greatest discovery of the ages. But what if the technique also developed the total creative potential of every child, led to solving the problems of the economy, and eliminated the basis of crime, violence, terrorism, and war? It would be hailed as greater than the greatest knowledge; it would be understood to give us Total Knowledge.

This is the fortunate situation we find ourselves in today as the old principles of fragmented, "fact-based" education are replaced by the new principles of Consciousness-Based education. We are entering the post–Information Age, where the experience of Total Knowledge will naturally lead to the prevention and solution of problems that have plagued humanity since time immemorial.

What is Total Knowledge?

I am often asked, "What is meant by Total Knowledge? Does it mean that you have a billion fragmented facts and figures buzzing around in your head?" The answer is no. Knowledge is not gained merely by acquiring facts; experience is also necessary for knowledge to be complete. For example, if someone tells you about a strawberry, you can't fully know what it is until you've had the taste of it.

Now, it is not possible to become knowledgeable about every discipline in one lifetime. Fortunately, however, Total Knowledge can be gained through the Science of Creative Intelligence,® which provides intellectual understanding and experience of the infinite potential of the Self.

Think of a seed. A single seed contains the total knowledge of everything about the tree. Like that, Maharishi explains, the Self—the Unified Field—which is open to direct experience through the Transcendental Meditation and TM-Sidhi programs, including Yogic Flying, contains Total Knowledge of everything in the universe.

Total Knowledge is the unified state of knowledge: the unified state of knower, knowing, and known. It is the experience of all the laws of nature in their fully unified state at a single point. And just as a child flies a kite by holding the string at one single point and controlling all the kite's dynamic activity from there, the experience of Total

Knowledge gives command over all the laws of nature in one single awareness.

According to Maharishi, this experience of Total Knowledge results in spontaneous right action—action supported by Natural Law*—so that people do not make mistakes and create problems either for themselves or for others. Desires are spontaneously evolutionary—of maximum benefit to the individual and the environment. And because desires are fully supported by Natural Law, they are fulfilled by mere intention—not by hard work, but by "soft thought"—more refined, more powerful levels of thinking. This is life in enlightenment.

If ignorance is defined as lack of knowledge, then only Total Knowledge can eliminate all ignorance. This is why we can call the knowledge offered by Consciousness-Based education Total Knowledge.

Old and new principles of education

While an education that provides fragmented knowledge leads to partial brain development, education that provides the experience of Total Knowledge leads to total brain development. Every day I marvel at the benefits this experience brings to the lives of the students. It is the proof that education everywhere should adopt the new principles of Consciousness-Based education.

---

*In the language of religion, action supported by Natural Law could be described as action in accord with the will of God.

What follows are some examples of these new principles, together with old principles that are rapidly becoming obsolete. By providing students with the experience of Total Knowledge, old principles get replaced by new principles spontaneously, just as the principles that govern living in a darkened room get replaced by new ones when someone discovers how to turn on the light.

Old Principle:
Education offers fragmented knowledge

Education can only offer students specialized knowledge of a few disciplines. This partial, fragmented approach leads to partial, fragmented brain development and inevitable problems and suffering in life.

New Principle:
Education offers holistic knowledge

Education provides students with holistic knowledge through the experience of Transcendental Consciousness— the unified basis of all knowledge. This experience enlivens the holistic functioning of the total brain physiology, which is necessary for a healthy, happy, progressive, fulfilled life—free from problems and suffering.

Old Principle:
Education is for gaining knowledge

Every year students gain some knowledge, but they become aware of a greater field of knowledge—unknown knowledge—lying ahead. In this way, modern education increases ignorance more than knowledge.

New Principle:
Education is for gaining Total Knowledge

Only Total Knowledge can eliminate all ignorance. Students continue to increase in knowledge every year until they gain Total Knowledge. This is possible because Consciousness-Based education connects the parts of knowledge to the totality of knowledge, which is structured in consciousness at the source of thought.

Old Principle:
Emphasis on the known

Education is geared to gaining knowledge of facts—the known.

New Principle:
Emphasis on the knower

Education is geared to gaining knowledge of the knower, thereby unfolding complete knowledge of the knower, process of knowing, and known.

Old Principle:
Emphasis on book knowledge

Students gain partial knowledge of various disciplines, such as physics, engineering, literature, etc., from books written by authors who are unaware of the totality of knowledge. Hence, students spend their time studying the restricted channels of other people's thought.

New Principle:
Emphasis on Self-knowledge

Students explore the full range of their own thought by taking their awareness to Transcendental Consciousness at the source of thought—the Self of every individual—and discovering Total Knowledge within their own consciousness. This is what education means—unfolding the totality of knowledge that is transcendental, hidden from view, within everyone.

Old Principle:
Education is information based

Information-based education overburdens children with innumerable facts. It puts them on an endless quest for knowledge in which the thirst for knowledge is never satisfied.

New Principle:
Education is consciousness based

Education continues to provide up-to-date information but also provides experience of Transcendental Consciousness—the Unified Field of All the Laws of Nature—at the source of thought. Experience of the home of all knowledge satisfies the thirst for knowledge and ensures that children grow to enjoy the fruit of all knowledge—a mistake-free life with maximum achievement and fulfillment.

Old Principle:
Work hard to accomplish more

In an attempt to make students successful, education subjects them to a lot of hard work geared toward training them for more hard work in the job market. But rather than providing them with a life of happiness and success, this approach generally leads to increased stress and exhaustion, leaving their success and good fortune dependent upon the ups and downs of the economy.

New Principle:
Do less and accomplish more

Schools offer students the simple, effortless Transcendental Meditation technique to provide experience of the source of thought—the source of their total creative potential. Instead of hard work, students fulfill their desires from the level of "soft thought"—more refined thinking. "Do less and accomplish more" is the formula for success in life.

Old Principle:
Enjoy 100% of life

Education focuses primarily on skills deemed necessary to create material comfort in life. It does not emphasize programs that can prevent the rising levels of stress that jeopardize health and happiness and prevent full enjoyment of material life.

New Principle:
Enjoy 200% of life

Education cultures the ability to enjoy 200% of life—100% inner happiness and 100% outer material success. Life is happy, healthy, and prosperous—free from stress, problems, and suffering.

Old Principle:
Education will help solve problems

Education attempts to train students to be effective problem solvers. But clearly, schools have not produced a large crop of effective problem solvers; otherwise, the age-old problems of mankind would have disappeared long ago. Rather than preventing problems, such as disease, crime, and violence, modern education often contributes to these problems by only partially developing the brain physiology and subjecting students to high levels of stress.

New Principle:
Education will prevent problems

Education enlivens the total creative potential of every student, without inflicting stress or strain. Decreased stress in the life of the individual and society results in decreasing problems, just as darkness disappears with the onset of light.

Old Principle:
Genius is born, not made

Education tries to adapt to students' "natural abilities." It does not unfold the inner genius that is innate within everyone.

New Principle:
Every child has inner genius, but it has to be unfolded

Consciousness-Based education develops the total brain physiology, thereby unfolding the creative genius of every student.

Old principle:
Students receive an academic report card

Students frequently take exams to test their knowledge of the different academic disciplines and the results are recorded on their report card.

New Principle:
Students receive a brain integration report card

In addition to an academic report card, students receive a brain integration report card documenting the rising coherence of their brain waves as they grow to enlightenment.

Old Principle:
Good schools are for the best students

Entrance exams are commonplace to ensure that only the most intellectually gifted students are admitted to prestigious schools.

New Principle:
Good schools are for every student

Consciousness-Based education develops the total creative potential of every student. As the inner genius of every child is unfolded, every school will become a good school.

Old Principle:
All knowledge on one campus

Good universities take pride in offering a wide range of knowledge on one campus. However, students graduate with little knowledge of any of it.

New Principle:
All knowledge in one brain

Consciousness-Based education offers the student Total Knowledge. It changes the goal of education from "all knowledge on one campus" to "all knowledge in one brain." Only this approach can deliver the "fruit of all knowledge"—mistake-free life in enlightenment for every human being.

Old Principle:
Schools attempt to culture ideal citizens

Schools attempt to culture ideal citizens by developing the whole student—mind, body, and spirit. However, the anti-social behavior prevalent in schools and in society proves that this goal is not easy to accomplish through the fragmented approach to knowledge offered in schools today.

New Principle:
Schools radiate peace and harmony for all citizens

Schools culture ideal citizenship by providing students with the experience of the Unified Field of All the Laws of Nature, thereby bringing the life of the student spontaneously into harmony with Natural Law—life in enlightenment. Groups of students practicing the Transcendental Meditation and TM-Sidhi program, including Yogic Flying, create a field effect—the Maharishi Effect—where peace and harmony are spontaneously radiated throughout society, leading to ideal citizenship for everyone, and invincibility for the nation.

11

Conclusion

For well over a decade, I have witnessed the students at Maharishi School growing daily in health, happiness, and success—toward higher states of consciousness. In this book I hope I have succeeded in conveying at least some of the excitement that these pioneers of Consciousness-Based education are generating in all areas of society—government, education, business, health, etc.

My experience is just one of many confirmations that Consciousness-Based education is the key to fulfilling the highest aspirations of students, parents, and teachers everywhere. Each year at graduation, I realize that every student has achieved something great while in high school. I love to hear the students' farewell speeches, and I never cease to marvel at how confident, articulate, wholesome, and successful they have become. They are students who feel at home with everyone and everything.

I have no doubt the graduates of Maharishi School will be the future leaders of the world. It is now time to give all children born in every country the same opportunity to realize their total creative potential.

I feel very fortunate that I have been given the opportunity to work at Maharishi School. Our school fulfills the students' desire to learn by offering Total Knowledge in contrast to the fragmented knowledge currently given in other schools. I hope this book has alerted you to the fact that a simple, practical solution to the problems plaguing information-based education is now available.

Every day, I witness the profound effects of Consciousness-Based education. This approach is not just book learning. It gives students the experience of their own Self—Transcendental Consciousness—which is the Unified Field of Natural Law, whose infinite creative potential administers the ever-expanding universe without a problem.

This experience brings unprecedented benefits for students—total brain development, increased alertness, full blossoming of creative intelligence, extraordinary academic achievements, more energy and better health, growth of inner peace and happiness, harmony with fellow students and teachers, and enlightened social behavior. And now students even have the opportunity to create and sustain peace in their community, nation, and world. All of these benefits have been confirmed by hundreds of scientific research studies.

> **Now students even have the opportunity to create and sustain peace in their community, nation, and world.**

Based on these results, and the successes already achieved at Maharishi School and at Consciousness-Based schools around the world, we can look forward to a bright future for humanity. We will see what responsible leaders have always wished for—happy, healthy, fulfilled individuals, and increasingly positive trends in society, where children respect their parents and teachers and satisfy their thirst for knowledge in schools and communities that are peaceful and harmonious.

The population will be healthier, and life will be lived free from stress, strain, and the fear of conflict. Creativity and intelligence will flourish, leading to unrestricted progress, where every individual fulfills his or her highest aspirations in harmony with those of the community and the whole world family. Every individual will rise to enlightenment and every nation will enjoy invincibility.

As parents and educators, let's fulfill our responsibility to the coming generation and offer Consciousness-Based education in our schools as soon as possible, so that every child born on earth can unfold Total Knowledge and realize the birthright of his or her total creative potential. We have the knowledge. All we have to do now is apply it.

"Trends in society will spontaneously be positive, progressive, and fulfilling. Negative tendencies of sickness, crime, and other weaknesses will naturally fall off, saving national energy and resources to structure the steps of fulfilling progress. Accidents and conflicts will disappear; morals and virtues will grow freely, and pure consciousness will guide the destiny of society for all good to everyone."

—*Maharishi*

Appendices

I

The Science of Creative Intelligence and the Fulfillment of Modern Science

Modern sciences are objective sciences, in which theory is confirmed by systematic, repeatable experiments. However, the unified level of nature's functioning lies beyond the domain of objective experimentation.

This leaves modern science knocking at the door of the Unified Field but unable to open it and experience the ultimate level of nature directly. Physicists can only search for indirect evidence of the Unified Field, such as supersymmetric particles, imprinted in the structure of the universe.

In attempting to study the Unified Field, the science of physics transcends its own validity. Rather than being a predominantly objective approach that confirms theory with direct observation, Unified Field physics is predominantly subjective, where physicists rely on their intellectual prowess (a subjective aspect of consciousness) to formulate mathematical constructs of the Unified Field that can never be directly confirmed by objective observation.

This dilemma arises because modern physics fails to take into account that the Unified Field, being the single unified source of everything in the universe, is the unified foundation of both subjective and objective existence. It is the unified state of the knower, process of knowing, and the known—a state of pure consciousness.

The Science of Creative Intelligence of Maharishi Mahesh Yogi offers fulfillment to science by offering a systematic technology of consciousness, the Transcendental Meditation technique, to allow anyone to research the Unified Field on its own level—the level of Transcendental Consciousness at the source of thought. (See Figure 7.) This systematic

Science

KNOWER
Subjective Approach

TRANSCENDENTAL MEDITATION ALLOWS THE CONSCIOUS MIND TO IDENTIFY ITSELF WITH THE UNIFIED FIELD OF ALL THE LAWS OF NATURE, THE TOTAL POTENTIAL OF NATURAL LAW, IN TRANSCENDENTAL CONSCIOUSNESS.

TRANSCENDENTAL CONSCIOUSNESS

UNIFIED FIELD
Unified State

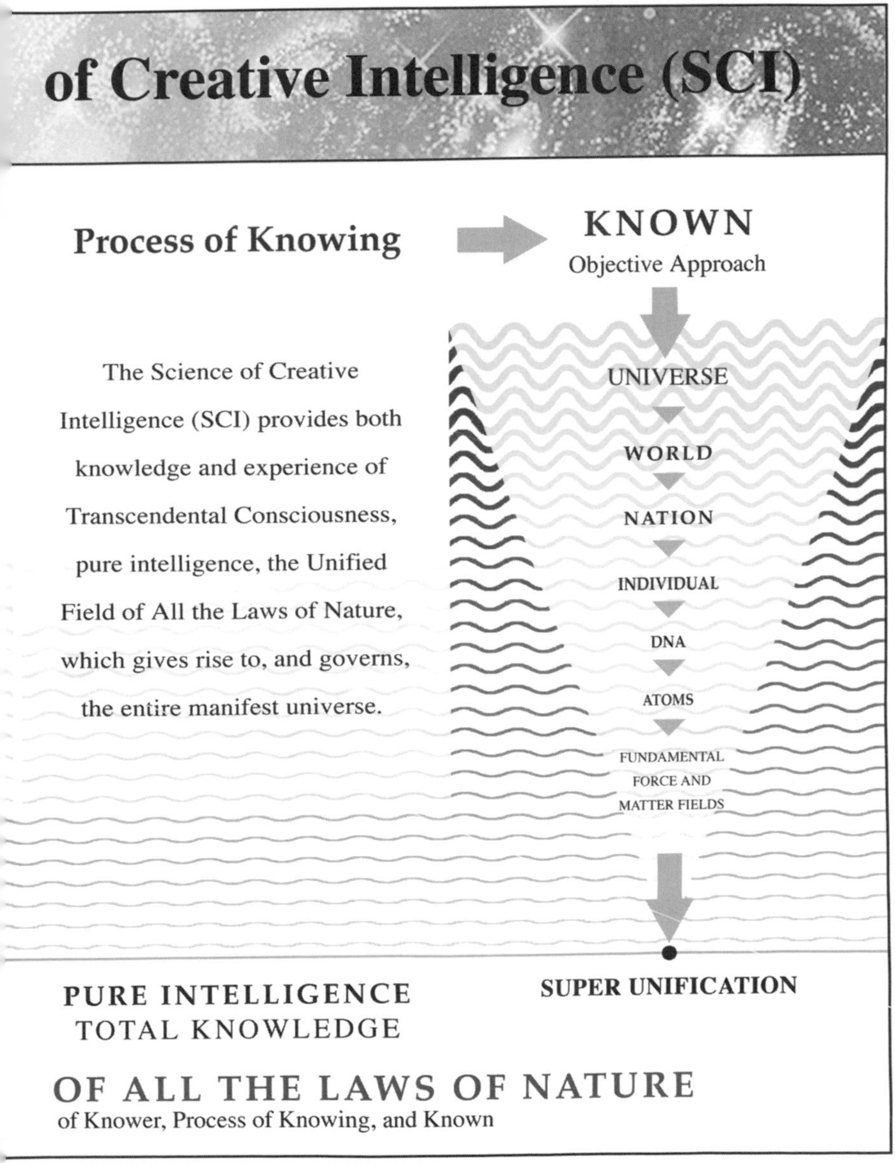

# of Creative Intelligence (SCI)

Process of Knowing ➡ KNOWN
Objective Approach

The Science of Creative Intelligence (SCI) provides both knowledge and experience of Transcendental Consciousness, pure intelligence, the Unified Field of All the Laws of Nature, which gives rise to, and governs, the entire manifest universe.

UNIVERSE
▼
WORLD
▼
NATION
▼
INDIVIDUAL
▼
DNA
▼
ATOMS
▼
FUNDAMENTAL
FORCE AND
MATTER FIELDS

SUPER UNIFICATION

PURE INTELLIGENCE
TOTAL KNOWLEDGE
OF ALL THE LAWS OF NATURE
of Knower, Process of Knowing, and Known

Figure 7

technology allows consciousness to explore itself by itself and thereby to reveal its inner structure of Total Knowledge to itself.

The discovery of the unification of subjective and objective existence brings to light that everything in the universe, including human physiology, is an expression of consciousness*—that atoms are made of the same stuff that thoughts are made of. Through SCI, students come to realize that the structure of the objective universe comprises the reverberations of their own pure consciousness—their own Self. This is the realization of Unity Consciousness.

II

Maharishi University of Management

Maharishi School of the Age of Enlightenment is situated on the grounds of Maharishi University of Management, a private college in southeast Iowa, founded by Maharishi in 1971. The mission of the University is to unfold the full creative potential of every student. Successful by any conventional measure—large research grants, accomplished graduates, and top placement in na-

*The great scientist, His Majesty Maharaja Nader Raam, first ruler of the Global Country of World Peace, received his weight in gold for his discovery that the human physiology is made of consciousness. (See Further Reading, Appendix III.)

tional surveys—the University's uniqueness is its ability to profoundly develop the total creative potential of the students.

Students practice the Transcendental Meditation and TM-Sidhi programs—techniques shown to increase creativity and awaken latent reserves in the brain. Students display increased intelligence and heightened alertness in the classroom, together with greater enjoyment of all that they learn.

The curriculum has been designed to make knowledge deeply relevant. Innovative classroom approaches connect all pieces of information to the wholeness of a student's own consciousness. According to seniors' responses on the National Survey of Student Engagement, Maharishi University of Management has one of America's most highly engaging approaches to education.

Academic programs

Maharishi University of Management offers a range of bachelor's, master's, and doctoral programs in the arts, sciences, humanities, and business. In addition to the traditional majors, special programs such as Environmental Science, Digital Media, Maharishi Consciousness-Based Health Care, and Maharishi Vedic Science are also offered.

Courses are taught on the block system, in which students take one course at a time. By fully immersing themselves in a subject, students gain knowledge with greater ease and enjoyment.

Faculty

Courses are taught personally by highly qualified faculty, including internationally recognized scholars and researchers with degrees from Oxford, Harvard, MIT, Stanford, and dozens of other leading universities. What sets the professors apart is their profound, holistic approach to their subjects. Their research, funded by over $18 million in federal and other grants, has included breakthrough discoveries in physics as well as new approaches to combating cancer, hypertension, and heart disease.

Accreditation

The university is accredited by The Higher Learning Commission and is a member of the North Central Association of Colleges and Schools (www.ncacihe.org).

Campus

The campus is located 50 miles west of the Mississippi River on a 272-acre campus in southeast Iowa. The environment is lively and diverse, drawing students from over 90 countries and from a range of religious backgrounds.

III

How to Learn
the *Transcendental Meditation* Technique

1) **Introductory Lecture:** A vision of possibilities through the Transcendental Meditation program (1 hour)

2) **Preparatory Lecture:** The mechanics and origin of the Transcendental Meditation technique (1 hour)

3) **Personal Interview:** A short meeting with a teacher of the Transcendental Meditation technique (15 minutes)

4) **Personal Instruction:** Learning the technique (1 hour)

5) **Verification and Validation of Experiences:** Verifying the correctness of the practice (90 minutes)

6) **Verification and Validation of Experiences:** Understanding the mechanics of stabilizing the benefits of the Transcendental Meditation technique (90 minutes)

7) **Verification and Validation of Experiences:** Understanding the mechanics of the development of higher states of consciousness through the Transcendental Meditation technique (90 minutes)

Contact information:

• To find a qualified teacher of the Transcendental Meditation program in your area, call 1-888-LEARNTM or visit www.tm.org

- To begin a program in your local school, contact the Consciousness-Based Education Association at www.cbeprograms.org

- For information on Maharishi Peace Palaces, visit www.globalcountry.org

- For more information on Yogic Flying Clubs, visit www.yogicflyingclubs.org

- For information on specific Consciousness-Based schools and universities:
  - Maharishi School of the Age of Enlightenment (day school and boarding school), Fairfield, IA USA: www.maharishischooliowa.org
  - Maharishi University of Management, Fairfield, IA, USA: www.mum.edu
  - Ideal Girls School, Maharishi Vedic City, IA, USA: www.idealgirlsschool.org
  - Ideal Girls School, Bethesda, MD, USA www.bethesdapeacepalace.org
  - Maharishi School, Melbourne, Australia: www.maharishischool.vic.edu.au

Further Reading

The following books are available from Maharishi University of Management Press (800-831-6523, www.mumpress.com) 1000 North 4th St., DB1155, Fairfield, IA 52557, USA:

- *Celebrating Perfection in Education*, Maharishi Mahesh Yogi

- *Discovery of Veda and Vedic Literature in Human Physiology*, His Majesty Maharaja Nader Raam

- *Maharishi Speaks to Educators*, Maharishi Mahesh Yogi

- *Maharishi Speaks to Students*, Maharishi Mahesh Yogi

- *Vedic Knowledge for Everyone*, Maharishi Mahesh Yogi

- *Science of Being and Art of Living*, Maharishi Mahesh Yogi

- *Manual for a Perfect Government*, John Hagelin, Ph.D.

- *Transcendental Meditation*, Robert Roth

- *Scientific Research on the Transcendental Meditation Program: Collected Papers*, Volumes 1–6

IV

About the Author

As far back as I can remember, I have loved to travel. Maybe it was trips to the ocean by steam train or traveling on London's underground, but I never doubted that someday I would be involved in something exciting. At age 4, in nursery school, I remember the teacher asking us what we wanted to be when we grew up. I couldn't answer because I wanted to do everything.

By age 15 I had decided to become a pilot in the Royal Air Force. I received my pilot's license while still in high school and joined the London University Air Squadron while studying physics at Imperial College. I loved the flying but found the physics a little dry. I still wanted to know everything and do everything, and while I found the flying exhilarating, the physics seemed to focus on obscure details with no obvious relevance to my life. However, when we began studying astronomy and astrophysics in my final year, I began to feel challenged by the big questions in life, such as "How did the universe start?" and "What is my place in it?"

After graduation, I decided to forgo a career in the Royal Air Force and pursue higher degrees in physics. While completing my Ph.D. in space science from York University in Toronto, I gradually began to realize that physics alone was not fulfilling my scientific quest to know more about how and why the universe began.

The path to gaining knowledge seemed interminable, with each experiment taking years and revealing only a small fraction of what remained to be discovered. I remember one day asking a friend about the spectrum of the nitric oxide molecule, to which he replied, "Sorry, that's not my molecule." I certainly didn't seem to be fulfilling my desire to know everything and do everything.

Then I learned the Transcendental Meditation technique. I found that the effects were immediate and very real. The first changes I noticed were physiological. I was less tired when I got up in the morning. Then I found I could focus better while studying. Then I realized I was a lot happier. I was becoming more alert, more awake, and more creative—in short, I was growing in consciousness. Gradually, I began to realize that to have greater knowledge of my Self and my place in the universe, I needed to more fully develop these qualities that result from growth of consciousness.

It was around this time that I attended a science conference in Ottawa, Canada at which researchers were presenting their findings on the Transcendental Meditation technique. Maharishi Mahesh Yogi was the keynote speaker. During his address, it dawned on me that Maharishi was unfolding knowledge that had been missing from my education—the scientific understanding of human consciousness. The scientists presented research showing that the simple technique of Transcendental Meditation, a technique for the development of consciousness, provides a means to address previously intractable problems in such diverse fields as education, health, crime prevention and rehabilitation, and international relations.

After completing my Ph.D., I traveled to Europe to take a course to become a teacher of the Transcendental Meditation program. There I met scientists who were thinking along the same lines as I was. It was becoming clear to me that consciousness holds the key to understanding the universe and our place in it.

After teaching the Transcendental Meditation program in Canada for several years, I joined the physics department at Maharishi University of Management. There I did research on Unified Field theories and their relationship to the structure of consciousness.

After seven years, I was offered the job of director of Maharishi School of the Age of Enlightenment. Here was my chance to help children have the education that I had always wanted—an education that unfolds complete knowledge of the inner Self and the outer universe—Total Knowledge—for a fulfilling, productive, and successful life.

References

(1) The National Information Center for Higher Education Policy Making and Analysis. Data for year 2000. www.higheredinfo.org

(2) U.S. Census Bureau. Data for year 2000.

(3) Amen, D. *Change Your Brain, Change Your Life*. Random House, New York, 1998.

(4) LoVette, O.K. and Jacob, S. Why do so many high achieving high school students dislike school? *NASSP Bulletin* 79: 70-75, 1995.

(5) Gardner, R. Jr. Poor little smart kids. *New York* 29: 30-37, 1996.

(6) Goodlad, J.I. *A Place Called School: Prospects for the Future*. McGraw-Hill, New York, 1984.

(7) Steinberg, L. et al. *Beyond the Classroom: Why School Reform Has Failed and What Parents Need To Do*, p. 67. Simon and Schuster, New York, 1996.

(8) Einstein, A. *Autobiographical Notes*, p. 15. Open Court, La Salle and Chicago, 1979.

(9) Bloom, A. *The Closing of the American Mind*, p. 339. Simon and Schuster, New York, 1987.

(10) Wallace, R.K. Physiological effects of Transcendental Meditation. *Science* 167: 1751-1754, 1970.

(11) Travis, F. Eyes open and TM EEG patterns after one and after eight years of TM practice. *Psychophysiology* 28 (3a): S58, 1991.

(12) Travis, F. et al. Patterns of EEG coherence, power, and contingent negative variation characterize the integration of transcendental and waking states. *Biological Psychology* 61: 293-319, 2002.

(13) Mason, L. et al. Electrophysiological correlates of higher states of consciousness during sleep in long-term practitioners of the Transcendental Meditation program. *Sleep* 20: 102-110, 1997.

(14) Ayer, A.J. *The Concept of a Person and Other Essays*, pp. 2-3. Macmillan, London, 1963.

(15) So, K.T. and Orme-Johnson, D.W. Three randomized experiments on the longitudinal effects of the Transcendental Meditation technique on cognition. *Intelligence* 29: 419-440, 2001.

(16) Nidich, S.I. et al. School effectiveness: Achievement gains at the Maharishi School of the Age of Enlightenment. *Education* 107: 49-54, 1986.

(17) Nidich, S.I. and Nidich, R.J. Increased academic achievement at Maharishi School of the Age of Enlightenment: A replication study. *Education* 109: 302-304, 1989.

(18) Hoffman, C. et al. Persons with chronic conditions: Their prevalence and costs. *Journal of the American Medical Association* 276: 1473-1479, 1996.

(19) The economic and budget outlook, 1998–2007. Congressional Budget Office. www.cbo.gov/showdoc.cfm?index=2&sequence=13

(20) Sapolsky, R.M. *Stress, the Aging Brain, and the Mechanisms of Neuron Death.* MIT Press, Cambridge, MA, 1992.

(21) Weiner, H. *Perturbing the Organism: The Biology of Stressful Experience.* University of Chicago Press, Chicago, IL, 1992.

(22) American Institute of Stress. www.stress.org/problem.htm

(23) Barnes, V.A. et al. Impact of Transcendental Meditation on ambulatory blood pressure in African-American adolescents. *American Journal of Hypertension* 17: 366-369, 2004.

(24) Barnes, V.A. et al. Impact of stress reduction on negative school behavior in adolescents. *Health and Quality of Life Outcomes* 1:10, 2003.

(25) Schneider, R.H. et al. A randomized controlled trial of stress reduction for hypertension in older African Americans. *Hypertension* 26: 820-827, 1995.

(26) Schneider, R.H. et al. A randomized controlled trial of stress reduction in the treatment of hypertension in African Americans during one year. *American Journal of Hypertension*, 18(1): 88-98, 2005.

(27) Orme-Johnson, D.W. Medical care utilization and the Transcendental Meditation program. *Psychosomatic Medicine* 49: 493-507, 1987.

(28) Orme-Johnson, D.W. and Herron, R.E. An innovative approach to reducing medical care utilization and expenditures. *The American Journal of Managed Care* 3: 135-144, 1997.

(29) Dillbeck, M.C. et al. The Transcendental Meditation program and crime rate change in a sample of forty-eight cities. *Journal of Crime and Justice* 4: 25-45, 1981.

(30) Dillbeck, M.C. et al. Test of a field model of consciousness and social change: The Transcendental Meditation and TM-Sidhi program and decreased urban crime. *The Journal of Mind and Behavior* 9: 457-486, 1988.

(31) Howeth, L.S. *History of Communications—Electronics in the United States Navy*, p. 11. U.S. Government Printing Office, Washington, D.C., 1963.

(32) Hagelin, J.S. Is consciousness the Unified Field? A field theorist's perspective. *Modern Science and Vedic Science* 1: 28-87, 1987.

(33) Cavanaugh, K.L. Time series analysis of U.S. and Canadian inflation and unemployment: A test of a field-theoretic hypothesis. *Proceedings of the American Statistical Association, Business and Economics Statistics Section* (Alexandria, VA: American Statistical Association): 799-804, 1987.

(34) Dillbeck, M.C. et al. Consciousness as a field: The Transcendental Meditation and TM-Sidhi program and changes in social indicators. *The Journal of Mind and Behavior* 8: 67-104, 1987.

(35) Cavanaugh, K.L. and King, K.D. Simultaneous transfer function analysis of Okun's misery index: Improvements in the economic quality of life through Maharishi's Vedic Science and technology of consciousness. *Proceedings of the American Statistical Association, Business and Economics Statistics Section* (Alexandria, VA: American Statistical Association): 491-496, 1988.

(36) Orme-Johnson, D.W. et al. International peace project in the Middle East: The effect of the Maharishi Technology of the Unified Field. *Journal of Conflict Resolution* 32: 776-812, 1988.

(37) Davies, J.L. Alleviating political violence through enhancing coherence in collective consciousness. *Dissertation Abstracts International* 49(8): 2381A, 1989.

(38) Dillbeck, M.C. Test of a field theory of consciousness and social change: Time series analysis of participation in the TM-Sidhi program and reduction of violent death in the U.S. *Social Indicators Research* 22: 399-418, 1990.

(39) Gelderloos, P. The dynamics of US–Soviet relations, 1979–1986: Effects of reducing social stress through the Transcendental Meditation and TM-Sidhi program. *Proceedings of the Social Statistics Section of the American Statistical Association* (Alexandria, VA: American Statistical Association): 297-302, 1990.

(40) Assimakis, P.D. and Dillbeck, M.C. Time series analysis of improved quality of life in Canada: Social change, collective consciousness, and the TM-Sidhi program. *Psychological Reports* 76: 1171-1193, 1995.

(41) Dillbeck, M.C. and Rainforth, M.V. Impact assessment analysis of behavioral quality of life indices: Effects of group practice of the Transcendental Meditation and TM-Sidhi program. *Proceedings of the Social Statistics Section of the American Statistical Association* (Alexandria, VA: American Statistical Association): 38-43, 1996.

(42) Hatchard, G.D. et al. The Maharishi Effect: A model for social improvement. Time series analysis of a phase transition to reduced crime in Merseyside metropolitan area. *Psychology, Crime, and Law* 2: 165-174, 1996.

(43) Hagelin, J.S. et al. Effects of group practice of the Transcendental Meditation program on preventing violent crime in Washington, DC: Results of the National Demonstration Project, June–July 1993. *Social Indicators Research* 47: 153-201, 1999.

(44) Orme-Johnson, D.W., et al. Preventing terrorism and international conflict: Effects of large assemblies of participants in the Transcendental Meditation and TM-Sidhi programs. *Journal of Offender Rehabilitation* 36: 283-302, 2003.

(45) Orme-Johnson, D.W. and Haynes, C.T. EEG phase coherence, pure consciousness, creativity, and TM-Sidhi experiences. *International Journal of Neuroscience* 13: 211-217, 1981.

(46) Dillbeck, M.C. et al. Frontal EEG coherence, H-reflex recovery, concept learning, and the TM-Sidhi program. *International Journal of Neuroscience* 15: 151-157, 1981.

Bibliography

Development of Full Mental Potential

Increased Creativity, Intelligence, and Learning Ability

Tjoa, A. Increased intelligence and reduced neuroticism through the Transcendental Meditation program. *Gedrag: Tijdschrift voor Psychologie* 3: 167-182, 1975.

Shecter, H.W. A psychological investigation into the source of the effect of the Transcendental Meditation technique. *Dissertation Abstracts International* 38(7): 3372B-3373B, 1978.

Travis, F. The Transcendental Meditation technique and creativity: A longitudinal study of Cornell University undergraduates. *Journal of Creative Behavior* 13: 169-180, 1979.

Aron, A. The Transcendental Meditation program in the college curriculum: A 4-year longitudinal study of effects on cognitive and affective functioning. *College Student Journal* 15: 140-146, 1981.

Dillbeck, M.C. et al. Frontal EEG coherence, H-reflex recovery, concept learning, and the TM-Sidhi program. *International Journal of Neuroscience* 15: 151-157, 1981.

Dillbeck, M.C. Meditation and flexibility of visual perception and verbal problem-solving. *Memory & Cognition* 10: 207-215, 1982.

Jedrczak, A. et al. The TM-Sidhi programme, pure consciousness, creativity and intelligence. *The Journal of Creative Behavior* 19: 270-275, 1985.

Dillbeck, M.C. et al. Longitudinal effects of the Transcendental Meditation and TM-Sidhi program on cognitive ability and cognitive style. *Perceptual and Motor Skills* 62: 731-738, 1986.

Jedrczak, A. et al. The TM-Sidhi programme, age, and brief test of perceptual-motor speed and nonverbal intelligence. *Journal of Clinical Psychology* 42: 161-164, 1986.

Warner, T.Q. Transcendental Meditation and developmental advancement: Mediating abilities and conservation performance. *Dissertation Abstracts International* 47(8): 3558B, 1987.

Dixon, C.A. Consciousness and cognitive development: A six-month longitudinal study of four-year-olds practicing the children's Transcendental Meditation technique. *Dissertation Abstracts International* 50(3): 1518B, 1989.

Cranson, R.W. et al. Transcendental Meditation and improved performance on intelligence-related measures: A longitudinal study. *Personality and Individual Differences* 12: 1105-1116, 1991.

So, K.T. and Orme-Johnson, D.W. Three randomized experiments on the longitudinal effects of the Transcendental Meditation technique on cognition. *Intelligence* 29: 419-440, 2001.

Higher Levels of Brain Functioning

Bennett, J.E. and Trinder, J. Hemispheric laterality and cognitive style associated with Transcendental Meditation. *Psychophysiology* 14: 293-296, 1977.

Banquet, J.P. and Lesevre, N. Event-related potentials in altered states of consciousness: Motivation, motor and sensory processes of the brain. *Progress in Brain Research* 54: 447-453, 1980.

McEvoy, T.M. et al. Effects of meditation on brainstem auditory evoked potentials. *International Journal of Neuroscience* 10: 165-170, 1980.

Warshal, D. Effects of the Transcendental Meditation technique on normal and Jendrassik reflex time. *Perceptual and Motor Skills* 50: 1103-1106, 1980.

Orme-Johnson, D.W. and Haynes, C.T. EEG phase coherence, pure consciousness, creativity, and TM-Sidhi experiences. *International Journal of Neuroscience* 13: 211-217, 1981.

Nidich, S.I. et al. Kohlbergian cosmic perspective responses, EEG coherence, and the Transcendental Meditation and TM-Sidhi program. *Journal of Moral Education* 12: 166-173, 1983.

Wallace, R.K. et al. Modification of the paired H reflex through the Transcendental Meditation and TM-Sidhi program. *Experimental Neurology* 79: 77-86, 1983.

Gallois, P. Modifications neurophysiologiques et respiratoires lors de la pratique des techniques de relaxation. *L'Encéphale* 10: 139-144, 1984.

Goddard, P.H. Reduced age-related declines of P300 latency in elderly practicing Transcendental Meditation. *Psychophysiology* 26: 529, 1989.

Cranson, R. et al. P300 under conditions of temporal uncertainty and filter attenuation: Reduced latency in long-term practitioners of TM. *Psychophysiology* 27 (Suppl.): 4A (Abstract), 1990.

Travis, F. Eyes open and TM EEG patterns after one and after eight years of TM practice. *Psychophysiology* 28 (3a): S58, 1991.

Lyubimov, N.N. Electrophysiological characteristics of mobilization of hidden brain reserves. Abstracts, the International Symposium "Physiological and Biochemical Basis of Brain Activity" (St. Petersburg, Russia: Russian Academy of Science, Institute of the Human Brain): 5, 1994.

Travis, F. and Miskov, S. P300 latency and amplitude during eyes-closed rest and Transcendental Meditation practice. *Psychophysiology* 31: S67 (Abstract), 1994.

Travis, F. Patterns of EEG coherence, power, and contingent negative variation characterize the integration of transcendental and waking states. *Biological Psychology* 61: 293-319, 2002.

Improvements in Academics and School Behavior

Schecter, H.W. A psychological investigation into the source of the effect of the Transcendental Meditation technique. Dissertation Abstracts International 38(7): 3372B-3373B, 1978.

Kember, P. The Transcendental Meditation technique and postgraduate academic performance. *British Journal of Educational Psychology* 55: 164-166, 1985.

Nidich, S.I. et al. School effectiveness: Achievement gains at the Maharishi School of the Age of Enlightenment. *Education* 107: 49-54, 1986.

Nidich, S.I. and Nidich, R.J. Increased academic achievement at Maharishi School of the Age of Enlightenment: A replication study. *Education* 109: 302-304, 1989.

Barnes, V.A. et al. Impact of stress reduction on negative school behavior in adolescents. *Health and Quality of Life Outcomes* 1:10, 2003.

Benefits for Special and Remedial Education

McIntyre, M.E. et al. Transcendental Meditation and stuttering: A preliminary report. *Perceptual and Motor Skills* 39: 294 (Abstract), 1974.

Allen, C.P. Effects of Transcendental Meditation, electromyographic (EMG) biofeedback relaxation, and conventional relaxation on vasoconstriction, muscle tension, and stuttering: A quantitative comparison. *Dissertation Abstracts International* 40(2): 689B, 1979.

Subrahmanyam, S. and Porkodi, K. Neurohumoral correlates of Transcendental Meditation. *Journal of Biomedicine* 1: 73-88, 1980.

Eyerman, J. Transcendental Meditation and mental retardation. *Journal of Clinical Psychiatry* 42: 35-36, 1981

Wood, M.F. The effectiveness of Transcendental Meditation as a means of improving the echolalic behavior of an autistic student. Paper presented at the International Symposium on Autism Research, Boston, Massachusetts, July 1981.

Improved Physical and Mental Health

Reduced Cadiovascular Disease Risk Factors

Schneider, R.H. et al. A randomized controlled trial of stress reduction for hypertension in older African Americans. *Hypertension* 26: 820-827, 1995.

Walton, K.G. et al. Psychosocial stress and cardiovascular disease, Part 2: Effectiveness of the Transcendental Meditation program in treatment and prevention. *Behavioral Medicine* 28: 106-123, 2002.

Barnes, V.A. et al. Impact of Transcendental Meditation on ambulatory blood pressure in African-American adolescents. *American Journal of Hypertension* 17: 366-369, 2004.

Schneider, R.H. et al. A randomized controlled trial of stress reduction in the treatment of hypertension in African Americans during one year. *American Journal of Hypertension*, 18(1): 88-98, 2005.

Decreased Medical Care Utilization and Hospitalization

Orme-Johnson, D.W. Medical care utilization and the Transcendental Meditation program. *Psychosomatic Medicine* 49: 493-507, 1987.

Haratani, T. and Hemmi, T. Effects of Transcendental Meditation (TM) on the mental health of industrial workers. *Japanese Journal of Industrial Health* 32: 656, 1990.

Haratani, T. and Hemmi, T. Effects of Transcendental Meditation (TM) on the health behavior of industrial workers. *Japanese Journal of Public Health* 37 (10 Suppl.): 729, 1990.

Herron, R.E. et al. The impact of the Transcendental Meditation program on government payments to physicians in Quebec. *American Journal of Health Promotion* 10: 208-216, 1996.

Orme-Johnson, D.W. and Herron, R.E. An innovative approach to reducing medical care utilization and expenditures. *The American Journal of Managed Care* 3: 135-144, 1997.

Decreased Anxiety and Faster Recovery from Stress

Orme-Johnson, D.W. Autonomic stability and Transcendental Meditation. *Psychosomatic Medicine* 35: 341-349, 1973.

Candelent, T. and Candelent, G. Teaching Transcendental Meditation in a psychiatric setting. *Hospital & Community Psychiatry* 26: 156-159, 1975.

Dillbeck, M.C. The effect of the Transcendental Meditation technique on anxiety level. *Journal of Clinical Psychology* 33: 1076-1078, 1977.

Brooks, J.S. and Scarano, T. Transcendental Meditation in the treatment of post-Vietnam adjustment. *Journal of Counseling and Development* 64: 212-215, 1985.

Eppley, K.R. et al. Differential effects of relaxation techniques on trait anxiety: A meta-analysis. *Journal of Clinical Psychology* 45: 957-974, 1989.

Gaylord, C. et al. The effects of the Transcendental Meditation technique and progressive muscle relaxation on EEG coherence, stress reactivity, and mental health in black adults. *International Journal of Neuroscience* 46: 77-86, 1989.

Alexander, C.N. et al. Effects of the Transcendental Meditation program on stress reduction, health, and employee development: A prospective study in two occupational settings. *Anxiety, Stress and Coping: An International Journal* 6: 245-262, 1993.

Reversal of Aging and Increased Longevity

Wallace, R.K. et al. The effects of the Transcendental Meditation and TM-Sidhi program on the aging process. *International Journal of Neuroscience* 16: 53-58, 1982.

Alexander, C.N. et al. Transcendental Meditation, mindfulness, and longevity. *Journal of Personality and Social Psychology* 57: 950-964, 1989.

Schneider, R.H. et al. Long-term effects of stress reduction on mortality in persons > 55 years of age with systemic hypertension. *American Journal of Cardiology* 95: 1060-1064, 2005.

Improved Social Behavior

Increased Efficiency, and Improved Integration of Personality

Seeman, W. et al. Influence of Transcendental Meditation on a measure of self-actualization. *Journal of Counseling Psychology* 19: 184-187, 1972.

Nidich, S. et al. Influence of Transcendental Meditation: A replication. *Journal of Counseling Psychology* 20: 565-566, 1973.

Appelle, S. and Oswald, L.E. Simple reaction time as a function of alertness and prior mental activity. *Perceptual and Motor Skills* 38: 1263-1268, 1974.

Frew, D.R. Transcendental Meditation and productivity. *Academy of Management Journal* 17: 362-368, 1974.

Pelletier, K.R. Influence of Transcendental Meditation upon autokinetic perception. *Perceptual and Motor Skills* 39: 1031-1034, 1974.

Holt, W.R. et al. Transcendental Meditation vs. pseudo-meditation on visual choice reaction time. *Perceptual and Motor Skills* 46: 726, 1978.

Gelderloos, P. Cognitive orientation toward positive values in advanced participants of the TM and TM-Sidhi program. *Perceptual and Motor Skills* 64: 1003-1012, 1987.

Gelderloos, P. Field independence of students at Maharishi School of the Age of Enlightenment and a Montessori school. *Perceptual and Motor Skills* 65: 613-614, 1987.

Alexander, C.N. et al. Transcendental Meditation, self-actualization, and psychological health: A conceptual overview and statistical meta-analysis. *Journal of Social Behavior and Personality* 6: 189-247, 1991.

Reduced Substance Abuse

Wallace, R.K. et al. Decreased drug abuse with Transcendental Meditation: A study of 1,862 subjects. In *Drug Abuse: Proceedings of the International Conference*, ed. Chris J.D. Zarafonetis (Philadelphia: Lea and Febiger): 369-376, 1972.

Shafii, M. et al. Meditation and marijuana. *American Journal of Psychiatry* 131: 60-63, 1974.

Shafii, M. et al. Meditation and the prevention of alcohol abuse. *American Journal of Psychiatry* 132: 942-945, 1975.

Monahan, R.J. Secondary prevention of drug dependence through the Transcendental Meditation program in metropolitan Philadelphia. *The International Journal of the Addictions* 12: 729-754, 1977.

Aron, E.N. and Aron, A. The patterns of reduction of drug and alcohol use among Transcendental Meditation participants. *Bulletin of the Society of Psychologists in Addictive Behaviors* 2: 28-33, 1983.

Alexander, C.N. et al. Treating and preventing alcohol, nicotine, and drug abuse through Transcendental Meditation: A review and statistical meta-analysis. *Alcoholism Treatment Quarterly* 11: 13-87, 1994.

Effective Criminal Rehabilitation

Abrams, A.I. and Siegel, L.M. The Transcendental Meditation program and rehabilitation at Folsom State Prison: A cross-validation study. *Criminal Justice and Behavior* 5: 3-20, 1978.

Bleick, C.R. and Abrams, A.I. The Transcendental Meditation program and criminal recidivism in California. *Journal of Criminal Justice* 15: 211-230, 1987.

Alexander, C.N. et al. Transcendental Meditation in criminal rehabilitation and crime prevention. *Journal of Offender Rehabilitation* 36 (1/2/3/4): 2003.

The Maharishi Effect: Reduced Crime

Dillbeck, M.C. et al. The Transcendental Meditation program and crime rate change in a sample of forty-eight cities. *Journal of Crime and Justice* 4: 25-45, 1981.

Dillbeck, M.C. et al. Test of a field model of consciousness and social change: The Transcendental Meditation and TM-Sidhi program and decreased urban crime. *The Journal of Mind and Behavior* 9: 457-486, 1988

The Maharishi Effect: Reduced Crime and Conflict, and Improved Economic and Social Trends

Cavanaugh, K.L. Time series analysis of U.S. and Canadian inflation and unemployment: A test of a field-theoretic hypothesis. *Proceedings of the American Statistical Association, Business and Economics Statistics Section* (Alexandria, VA: American Statistical Association): 799-804, 1987.

Dillbeck, M.C. et al. Consciousness as a field: The Transcendental Meditation and TM-Sidhi program and changes in social indicators. *The Journal of Mind and Behavior* 8: 67-104, 1987.

Cavanaugh, K.L. and King, K.D. Simultaneous transfer function analysis of Okun's misery index: Improvements in the economic quality of life through Maharishi's Vedic Science and technology of consciousness. *Proceedings of the American Statistical Association, Business and Economics Statistics Section* (Alexandria, VA: American Statistical Association): 491-496, 1988.

Orme-Johnson, D.W. et al. International peace project in the Middle East: The effect of the Maharishi Technology of the Unified Field. *Journal of Conflict Resolution* 32: 776-812, 1988.

Davies, J.L. Alleviating political violence through enhancing coherence in collective consciousness. *Dissertation Abstracts International* 49(8): 2381A, 1989.

Dillbeck, M.C. Test of a field theory of consciousness and social change: Time series analysis of participation in the TM-Sidhi program and reduction of violent death in the U.S. *Social Indicators Research* 22: 399-418, 1990.

Gelderloos, P. et al. The dynamics of US–Soviet relations, 1979–1986: Effects of reducing social stress through the Transcendental Meditation and TM-Sidhi program. *Proceedings of the Social Statistics Section of the American Statistical Association* (Alexandria, VA: American Statistical Association): 297-302, 1990.

Assimakis, P.D. and Dillbeck, M.C. Time series analysis of improved quality of life in Canada: Social change, collective consciousness, and the TM-Sidhi program. *Psychological Reports* 76: 1171-1193, 1995.

Dillbeck, M.C. and Rainforth, M.V. Impact assessment analysis of behavioral quality of life indices: Effects of group practice of the Transcendental Meditation and TM-Sidhi program. *Proceedings of the Social Statistics Section of the American Statistical Association* (Alexandria, VA: American Statistical Association): 38-43, 1996.

Hatchard, G.D. et al. The Maharishi Effect: A model for social improvement. Time series analysis of a phase transition to reduced crime in Merseyside metropolitan area. *Psychology, Crime, and Law* 2: 165-174, 1996.

Hagelin, J.S. et al. Effects of group practice of the Transcendental Meditation program on preventing violent crime in Washington, DC: Results of the National Demonstration Project, June-July 1993. *Social Indicators Research* 47: 153-201, 1999.

Orme-Johnson, D.W., et al. Preventing terrorism and international conflict: Effects of large assemblies of participants in the Transcendental Meditation and TM-Sidhi programs. *Journal of Offender Rehabilitation* 36: 283-302, 2003.

Consciousness and the Unified Field

Hagelin, J.S. Is consciousness the Unified Field? A field theorist's perspective. *Modern Science and Vedic Science* 1: 28-87, 1987.